Priority Setting in Action

purchasing dilemmas

Frank Honigsbaum
Senior Research Fellow
Health Services Management Centre
University of Birmingham

John Richards
Strategic Planner
Southampton and South West Hampshire
Health Commission

Tony Lockett
Head of Financial Planning and Health Economics
Southampton and South West Hampshire
Health Commission

Foreword by Chris Ham
Health Services Management Centre
University of Birmingham

RADCLIFFE MEDICAL PRESS
Oxford and New York

© 1995 Frank Honigsbaum, John Richards and Tony Lockett

Radcliffe Medical Press Ltd
18 Marcham Road, Abingdon, Oxon OX14 1AA, UK

Radcliffe Medical Press, Inc.
141 Fifth Avenue, New York, NY 10010, USA

British Library Cataloguing in Publication Data

A catalogue record for this book is available from the British Library.

ISBN 1 85775 100 0

Library of Congress Cataloging-in-Publication Data is available.

Typeset by Marksbury Typesetting Ltd, Midsomer Norton, Bath, UK
Printed and bound by Biddles Ltd., Guildford and King's Lynn

Contents

5   Outstanding issues   139

List of contributors

Nick Allen
Director of Health Strategy and Public Health
Southampton and South West Hampshire Health Commission

Jo Ash
Director
Southampton Council of Community Service

Brian Burdekin
Non-executive member
Southampton and South West Hampshire Health Commission

Irene Candy
Non-executive member
Southampton and South West Hampshire Health Commission

Len Doyal
Reader in Medical Ethics
The London Hospital and St. Bartholomew's Medical Colleges
University of London

Colin Godber
Consultant in Old Age Psychiatry
Southampton Community Health Services Trust

Jack Howell
Chairman
Southampton and South West Hampshire Health Commission

Brian Irish
Non-executive member
Southampton and South West Hampshire Health Commission

Bob Lee
Non-executive member
Southampton and South West Hampshire Health Commission

Peter Lees
Senior Lecturer in Neurosurgery, Southampton University; Honorary
Consultant Neurosurgeon and Director of Research and Development
Southampton University Hospitals Trust

Tony Lockett
Head of Financial Planning and Health Economics
Southampton and South West Hampshire Health Commission

Lawrence Maule
GP Principal
Lymington, Hampshire

James Raftery
Wessex Institute of Public Health and the National Casemix Office
Honorary Senior Lecturer
Department of Public Health Sciences
Southampton Medical School

John Richards
Strategic Planner
Southampton and South West Hampshire Health Commission

Ray Robinson
Professor of Health Policy and Director of the Institute for Health
Policy Studies
University of Southampton

Brian Strevens
Non-executive member
Southampton and South West Hampshire Health Commission

Brian Irish
Non-executive member
Southampton and South West Hampshire Health Commission

Bob Lee
Non-executive member
Southampton and South West Hampshire Health Commission

Peter Lees
Senior Lecturer in Neurosurgery, Southampton University; Honorary
Consultant Neurosurgeon and Director of Research and Development
Southampton University Hospitals Trust

Tony Lockett
Head of Financial Planning and Health Economics
Southampton and South West Hampshire Health Commission

Lawrence Maule
GP Principal
Lymington, Hampshire

James Raftery
Wessex Institute of Public Health and the National Casemix Office
Honorary Senior Lecturer
Department of Public Health Sciences
Southampton Medical School

John Richards
Strategic Planner
Southampton and South West Hampshire Health Commission

Ray Robinson
Professor of Health Policy and Director of the Institute for Health
Policy Studies
University of Southampton

Brian Strevens
Non-executive member
Southampton and South West Hampshire Health Commission

Participants

A list of participants in Purchasing Dilemmas appears here. The exercise was devised by John Richards and Tony Lockett of Southampton and South West Hampshire Health Commission. They not only supplied the essential documents contained in this work but provided background information and contributed to the text. The 'experts' who appeared before the commission also contributed papers to the book with statements explaining their views.

The exercise was held at the Novotel in Southampton on 19 and 20 September 1994. It was conducted under the lead of Professor Chris Ham, who led the commission through the many stages involved in setting priorities. The reporter was Frank Honigsbaum, Senior Research Fellow at the Health Services Management Centre, University of Birmingham, which is under the direction of Professor Ham.

1   Members of the Southampton and South West Hampshire Health Commission

Professor JBL Howell (Chairman)
Mrs IF Candy (Vice Chairman)
Mr JB Burdekin (non-executive)
Professor CF George (non-executive)
Mr BI Irish (non-executive)
Dr R Lee (non-executive)
Reverend BL Strevens (non-executive)
Mr PA Shaw (Chief Executive)

Dr NA Allen (Director of Health Strategy and Public Health)
Mr L Judd (Director of Healthcare Commissioning and Primary Care)
Mr IV Marriott (Director of Finance, Information and Performance)
Mr AM Cochrane (Associate Director, Performance and Development)
Mrs A Jeffrey (Associate Director, Primary Care)
Mrs R Archer (Assistant Director, Social Services)
Mr J Whale (Chairman CHC – observer)

2   Health Services Management Centre, Birmingham University

Professor Chris Ham
Mr Frank Honigsbaum

3   Staff of the Southampton and South West Hampshire Health Commission

Mr John Richards
Dr Tony Lockett

4   Expert panel

Professor Ray Robinson
Ms Jo Ash
Dr Lawrence Maule
Dr James Raftery
Mr Peter Lees
Mr Len Doyal
Dr Colin Godber

5   Observers

- Representatives of the community health council
- Representatives of the four district councils
- Six students from Brockenhurst College
- Representatives of the NHS Executive (South and West)
- Representatives of Glaxo Pharmaceuticals plc, NHS Relations Division

Foreword

Priority setting is a pervasive feature of all health care systems. In the national health service (NHS), priority setting has become more transparent as a result of the separation of purchaser and provider responsibilities. In particular, health authorities, as the purchasers of services for their communities, are in the position of having to decide what services to purchase and how to translate this into contracts. To help in this process, health authorities have adopted a number of techniques to aid decision making. Much of this work is, however, at an early stage of development, and most decisions are shaped by history and inherited commitments. In so far as change does occur it tends to be at the margins and few health authorities have chosen to ration by excluding whole categories of care from their contracts.

Recognizing the complexity of priority setting, the Southampton and South West Hampshire Health Commission participated in a simulation exercise in 1991. The results of this exercise attracted widespread interest and highlighted a number of the issues involved in priority setting by health authorities in the new NHS. The Health Commission followed up this exercise in 1994 by taking time out to consider its priorities for the coming year. This book reports the outcome of this process. As the book illustrates, priority setting is an inherently complex activity and there are no easy solutions. Furthermore, given that there is no such thing as a correct list of priorities, the way in which decisions are made becomes particularly important. If health authorities can show that they have considered carefully alternative options and weighed evidence and views from different sources, it will be easier for them to justify their decisions.

The Southampton experience reported in this book contains some clues as to the approaches health authorities might pursue. As the editors and contributors make clear, not everything that was tried was successful and some important lessons were learnt in the process. This applies both to the consultation with stakeholders and the use of economics techniques. The difficulty of comparing and ranking a large number of options emerges as an important finding as does the challenge of operationalizing values such as equity and access in the decision making process. By presenting the results of their work, warts and all, the members of the health authority and the participants in the process provide an honest and illuminating account for others struggling with similar issues. If at the end of the story there is no tool kit to emerge for health authorities to apply in their own circumstances, then this in itself is an important conclusion. The need now is to refine the methods tested in Southampton and to build a more robust approach for the future. This has to recognize the inevitable messiness of priority setting and the absence of simple answers. In explaining how one district grapples with these issues, this book serves a useful purpose, not least in drawing out the lessons and implications for others.

Professor Chris Ham
Director
Health Services Management Centre
University of Birmingham

Preface

There is no such thing as a correct set of priorities, or even a correct way of setting priorities. However, we would at minimum expect district purchasers to establish approaches to decision making that are systematic; are transparent; take full account of the views of the public, health professionals and other interested parties; are based as far as possible on a firm assessment of need – taking full account of epidemiological data; and, where the information is available, make full use of effectiveness and cost-effectiveness data. (Para 67).

We have heard of many innovative ideas from purchasers; however, we have found it almost impossible to judge which of these approaches work, and which do not. . .If there are significant benefits to be gained, other purchasers should be aware of them. . .(Para 68).

Recommendations of the Health Committee First Report, *Priority Setting in the NHS: Purchasing*, Volume I, January 1995

Who decides on priorities in health care? Politicians, health managers, doctors or the public? How should it best be done? The demand for health care resulting from the burden of disease and our increasing ability to prevent or treat disease creates financial pressures which are forcing health planners throughout the world to find answers to these questions.

This book shows how priorities were set by one purchasing organization in the UK, the Southampton and South West Hampshire Health Commission. The subject is reviewed in detail, dealing with the difficult task of allocating resources efficiently across the whole range of health care.

Previous UK studies of priority setting have tended to involve simulations or limited experiments, focusing on ranking the treatments for a group of health problems (such as heart disease) or of allocating project funds. Southampton's role as a commissioning body, sitting astride primary and secondary health care and with a remit to secure better health for the local population, has led it to take a more holistic view of resource allocation, examining in its health strategy to the year 2000 how best to deploy the £230 million spent each year on its population of 455 000.

Recent studies, notably the work of David Cohen and colleagues in Mid-Glamorgan (*British Medical Journal* **309:** 781–5), suggest that there may be value in using methods borrowed from economics to aid decision making about priorities, in particular the techniques of programme budgeting and marginal analysis. In Southampton, we attempted to build on this experience, and this book will hopefully contribute significantly to our developing understanding, as commissioners, of which methods work best for our purposes.

The need to look at priority setting 'across' disease groups (e.g. between mental health and cancers), as well as 'within' them, is probably felt most sharply by commissioners for authorities in the major conurbations, who are facing, year on year, real losses in the funding available to them due to the introduction of capitation-based allocations. There, the need to look critically at how well resources are being used across the board is inescapable if the health gains desired for the population are to be achieved. Southampton has been more fortunate, each year receiving some 'growth' money to fund improvements. Nevertheless, the sense of taking the wider view is readily apparent and to avoid this, concentrating only on the use of 'growth' money, would be a dereliction of our duty.

Purchasing Dilemmas therefore represented an attempt to prioritize our new investments within a framework set by our health strategy. We were planning on an assumption of 2% real-terms growth. In practice, we have found a less rosy picture and have returned to look more purposefully at how we might scale down our funding of some services (or 'disinvest' from them) to enable us to invest in the top priorities for health gain.

Similar attempts to introduce rational planning methods have been made elsewhere, notably in the State of Oregon in the USA. There, the aim was more ambitious, to define a basic package of care, and elaborate methods were devised to pursue it. That and other experience formed a background to what was attempted in Southampton.

This book begins with a review of the international context. It then describes the Southampton experience and presents the lessons to be learned. Much remains to be done before a satisfactory way can be found to set priorities, and we would certainly not wish to claim that we have found the answer. However, we know that we have benefited greatly from our attempts and recommend that other commissioners sustain their efforts to refine the process.

The book concludes with some themes emerging from our endeavours which we believe are of wider relevance. Various authors contributed to these sections their personal views and speculations as to the future. In an environment of rapid change it is important that we continually reassess the relevance of what we do.

The members of the commission, non-executive and executive, deserve considerable credit for their involvement. Without their contributions and their willingness to be the subject of such public scrutiny, this exercise would not have been possible.

This book is an opportunity to share our experiences in this most difficult field which is central to our role as commissioners. We commend it to others in the knowledge that our dilemmas are not unique and our solutions far from perfect.

Tony Shaw, Chief Executive
Southampton and South West Hampshire Health Commission

1 The international context

Priorities have long been set in health care, but seldom in an explicit or public manner. They were applied mainly in private by clinicians in the way they treated patients. Priorities assumed public view only in the form of waiting lists for treatment or restrictions on access to services such as renal dialysis.

In recent years, attempts have been made to conduct the process more openly. The State of Oregon in the USA led the way and stimulated developments elsewhere.

The United Kingdom followed as the result of pressures emanating from the introduction of an internal market in 1991. The act of purchasing health care was separated from its provision, and that led parties on both sides of the process to look more critically at the decisions taken. Purchasing authorities, in particular, began searching for ways to make the most of the funds at their disposal. They found it both necessary and desirable to make priority setting methods known.

This section describes what has been learned thus far. The way priorities are set in five leading countries is assessed: Oregon in the USA, The Netherlands, New Zealand, Sweden and the United Kingdom. This is based mainly on a report of a seminar held in Stockholm in 1993 and published under the title *Priority Setting Processes for Healthcare*[1]. Additional information relating to Oregon has been obtained since.

Oregon

Oregon has set priorities across the whole spectrum of medical, dental and mental health care. An extensive list was prepared in the form of condition–treatment pairs covering all that health care could offer[2].The pairs were ranked in an order which, for the most part, put the most effective treatment at the top and the least effective at the bottom. The plan was devised to meet budget restrictions under America's Medicaid provision for the poor, a system run by the states but subject to federal regulation. It was left to the state legislature to decide how far down the list Oregon could afford to go. However, because most of the money came from Washington, federal approval was needed before the plan could go into effect. On the list finally approved, 565 of 696 items were funded. This began operating on 1 February 1994, and covered only medical and dental care. Mental health care, along with conditions relating to the elderly and disabled, were not added until 1 January 1995. This integrated list contains 745 items, of which 606 are funded.

Attempt to use QALYs

Oregon tried three methods before its plan was finally approved. The first was based strictly on cost–utility, using the cost per quality adjusted life year (QALY) technique. If, for example, treatment for a particular condition costs £1000 and is expected to last ten years, the cost per year would be £100. But if only five of those years were of acceptable quality, then the cost would be £200.

The cost per QALY figure was used to rank the pairs in priority order, and it produced so many anomalies that the plan was nearly abandoned. Cost and outcome data were lacking for most of the exercise. Only well-defined procedures, such as cardiac artery bypass grafts, could be reliably assessed.

Ranking based on categories of care

The next method was based on broad groupings of care which were ranked in priority order. At the top of the 17 categories employed came life-saving treatments with a good quality of life, followed by maternity care and preventive services for children. At the bottom was a category containing treatments which would have little or no effect on quality of life.

Condition–treatment pairs were fitted into these categories using an algorithm based mainly on varying rates of mortality and quality of well-being. For example, within the first category came fatal acute conditions with treatment resulting in at least a 25% reduction in mortality during the five years following treatment and with at least 90% of surviving patients returning to a very high quality of life.

Ranking within categories was carried out by a mathematical procedure similar to the one used earlier but with less weight attached to cost and more to duration of benefit and quality of well-being. This still left some services in an awkward position, and a 'reasonableness' test was used to adjust the rankings. So many hand adjustments were made that a large element of guesswork and judgement went into the final order.

Quality of life ruled out

This method failed to win federal approval because it violated the rights of disabled persons under an Act passed in 1990. All consideration of quality of life had to be removed from the ranking process and that, combined with pressure from user groups, led to the upgrading of several controversial procedures.

The category method of classification also had to be abandoned because quality of life considerations had been used to set the order in which they were ranked. In its place, a new method was devised which is unique to Oregon and not conducive to replication.

In Oregon as elsewhere, very few outcome data were available, and this meant that a large element of subjective judgement went into the process.

Those who compiled evidence of effectiveness did not have the time or resources to make extensive literature reviews, and many findings were based on the experience of local specialists in the conditions under consideration. The list is being modified as additional data become available.

Nevertheless, however inadequate Oregon methods were, the list at least provides a template against which specific services can be assessed. Though cultural differences may prevail, it can offer guidance to priority setting everywhere.

The plan was finally approved by the incoming Clinton administration subject to several conditions, the main one being that no further treatments could be removed without federal approval.

The plan in operation

The plan has appeared to work tolerably well since it began operating in February 1994. This may be partly due to the coverage of controversial items previously excluded. The list reflects a cautious approach to rationing. Hard choices have been avoided, so much so that one wonders whether the plan will achieve the aim of its prime movers to shift resources from acute to chronic and preventive care.

The plan may prove more controversial if further cuts are forthcoming. The State of Oregon faces severe budgetary problems, and more items may have to be removed from funding. Whether this will be accepted by the federal government is uncertain.

Financial pressure may also come from the addition of mental health services in 1995. All but eight of the 49 items added are funded, and the high cost of some could force further restrictions in list coverage.

Another problem may arise if the list is not effectively monitored. Services are being provided mainly by managed care organizations, which receive capitation payments based on the estimated cost of included treatments. But unless these providers supply detailed data on each item, it will not be possible to tell whether the treatments paid for are actually supplied.

Problems in methodology

The removal of quality of life considerations has far-reaching implications and was resented by those who prepared the Oregon plan. They would have preferred to operate the list which failed to win federal approval.

However, they may be ready to accept a modification in the way quality of life is gauged. In Oregon, disability assessments were not made by those who were disabled. In future, disability may be based on an average of the scores of those who are disabled and those who are not.

In place of QALYs, disability life years (DALYs) may be used. With QALYs, no value is given for the extra years of life at a lower quality; DALYs take account of full life expectancy or length of treatment effectiveness regardless of quality.

Clinicians may still withhold covered services if they judge outcome to be poor, and that assessment could include quality of life considerations. More explicit restrictions could be developed from the clinical guidelines being slowly formulated (a maximum of eight every two years) under legislative direction.

A major weakness of Oregon methodology was the failure to take account of needs assessment. The state, like America in general, has a serious obesity problem, yet the two services relating to obesity were not funded. Decisions were made largely on the basis of effectiveness, and trials relating to obesity procedures have not produced the necessary evidence. Yet the need for some form of treatment is so pressing that funding should have been forthcoming.

Public values were meant to inform decision making, and an impressive list was prepared, taken from community meetings. But the meetings were not representative of the public and no method was devised to relate values to ranking. Subjective judgements were used instead.

Equity was not given a high value ranking despite the fact that the main aim of the plan was to extend Medicaid coverage to all below the poverty level. This value, as well as community compassion, does not appear to be as strongly held in Oregon (or America generally) as elsewhere.

The Netherlands, New Zealand and Sweden

The Oregon plan has inspired priority setting efforts elsewhere, but development has been slower. The comprehensive list compiled in Oregon is the only one that covers all of health care.

Oregon may have been able to move more rapidly because its plan applies only to the poor. Elsewhere, whole populations are involved and public feeling for equity may be stronger than in America. In this section, we shall examine methods in The Netherlands, New Zealand and Sweden.

The Netherlands

Methods proposed here come closest to the Oregon model, but they have yet to be implemented. In 1992, an official committee called for the creation of a priority list on Oregon lines using four criteria to produce a basic package of care. Treatments would have to pass through the following sieves before they would be included:

- Is the care necessary from the community point of view?
- If so, has it been demonstrated to be effective?
- Is it also efficient, using such methods as QALYs?
- Can it still be left to individual responsibility?

Individual patients and doctors might take a different view of necessary care, but the committee called for the community approach in the first sieve. It defined health as the possibility for every member of society to function normally. This enabled it to stress services for the chronic sick and vulnerable groups such as the mentally ill. As in Oregon, the committee felt the need to curb high-technology treatment in the acute sector.

The second sieve could eliminate many treatments if applied strictly. Rigid tests of effectiveness apply to only a small proportion of health care. This could frustrate protection for the chronic sick and vulnerable groups since many of the services involved have yet to prove their worth.

The third sieve deals with cost–utility and will again be difficult to apply because of the limited data available.

The fourth sieve is a novel one and leaves some treatment to be financed by patients themselves.

The final package is not likely to be as restricted as these sieves suggest since it will be determined by political considerations. Compulsory insurance now covers only 60% of the population, but another government committee recommended that it be extended to everyone. Such a system would have to offer ample provision. The committee called for 85% of treatments to be included in the basic package, but even this was not enough for the government, and it raised the proportion to 95%.

Some action has been taken; but a basic care package still has to be defined. Public opinion has tended to resist service restriction, and a three-year programme has been proposed, aimed at influential consumer groups, to show the need for hard choices. This is one of the strongest features of the Dutch model and it has been implemented.

New Zealand

Here, methods deviated most sharply from Oregon. An official committee was asked to define an essential core of services but, in view of the country's long history of universal provision, it approached the subject cautiously. Existing services were assumed to be suitable but the committee thought changes might be made in the way resources were allocated. Before priority setting began, it suggested how services might be provided more efficiently, a procedure which Oregon did not follow.

The first task was to take an inventory of existing services, showing the volume and cost of the 20 most common conditions. The largest cost was due to normal childbirth which had bed stays twice the American average. If only one day were cut, that would be enough to build a 120-bed hospital.

Public opinion has opposed the creation of a priority list on the Oregon model, finding it complex, time-consuming, costly and divisive. In its place, the preference is for a general, positive list that would show in broad categories (such as mental, geriatric and children) the services that would be provided. Only a short negative list would be added, indicating services to be excluded. As elsewhere, public priorities favour a shift to prevention and chronic care, but it has proved difficult to secure agreement on which services to cut.

To show the need for choices to be made, the committee again took a cautious approach. The public was consulted without consideration given to whether services as such should be excluded. Instead, attention was focused on whether and when they should be offered. The key consideration was the benefit of 'a particular service to a particular person at a particular time'. This could provide more flexibility in service provision than the priority list prepared in Oregon.

Four questions were posed to make assessments:

- What are the benefits of a service?
- Is it value for money?
- Is it fair?
- Is it consistent with the community's values and priorities?

The most important and complex is the question of fairness. By comparing relative benefits, a way might be found of shifting resources across specialties, but it is proposed that this be done in small changes which do not shock the system.

More progress has been made on ways to provide existing services more appropriately. This has been done by the development of what are called *boundary* guidelines so as to stress the fact that they leave scope for clinician judgement. By working directly with clinicians to clarify when services should be provided and to whom, it will be possible for policy-makers progressively to identify those services which provide poor net benefit and to exclude them from publicly funded services, thus freeing up money for other priorities.

Sweden

Priority setting here has only just begun, and with health care under local authority control methods vary greatly. However, a central government commission has suggested how the process might proceed.

Three principles were proposed as a basis for priority setting:

1 Human dignity, or the need to treat everyone equally regardless of age, lifestyle or, in the case of premature babies, low birthweight. However, treatment could still be withheld if judged not to be of sufficient benefit. Patients who pay privately should be entitled only to amenities such as a private room, not a higher standard of care.

2 Solidarity, or the provision of resources to those who need them most, such as the mentally ill.

3 Efficiency, or treatment with the most cost-effective methods available, assuming all other considerations to be equal.

On the administrative level, resources would be allocated on the basis of needs, not the demands of those who shout the loudest. On the clinical level, decisions, as always, would be made by clinicians, but with essentially the same priorities as on the administrative level.

The commission set forth priorities in the form of categories reminiscent of those used in Oregon but fewer in number – five as opposed to 17. At the top came not only life-saving treatment for acute disease but care for vulnerable groups such as the mentally ill and those with severe chronic illness. At the bottom was treatment for minor ailments or that which would have little or no effect, such as for the terminally ill.

As in New Zealand, the commission declined to define a basic package, contending only that the vast majority of care should be funded. Also, Swedish authorities have yet to offer scope for public consultation as the politicians fear the consequences. This may be the country's greatest failing in the priority setting process.

Methods pursued at local level
The Oregon example inspired Swedish interest in priority setting, but thus far only one county council (Gavleborg) has started to prepare a detailed list. It is using four categories instead of 17, and conditions within categories are being classified by doctors from the specialties involved rather than by an independent body using an algorithm as in Oregon. In addition, in contrast to The Netherlands, Gavleborg recognizes the difficulty of proving effectiveness and will accept the existence of a wide consensus on the worth of treatment.

This procedure gives the doctors involved a chance to reach agreement on the priorities assigned, but the final decision will be made by the members of the county council. The politicians' role will not be restricted to funding as in Oregon, or deciding how far down the list the authority could afford to go.

Stockholm, by contrast, is looking at services in the form of 'bite-size chunks', such as cancer and heart disease. It wants to see how resources might be better distributed between prevention, treatment and rehabilitation. This approach was inspired by the seminar conducted at Southampton in 1991 (see pages 17–21). It recognizes that there is no simple way of setting priorities and that the task can only be done through a process of informed discussion.

However, problems have arisen similar to those faced in South-ampton. This method tends to focus attention on conditions for which reliable information is available and thus tends to concentrate on the acute rather than the chronic sick. Also, implementation has lagged behind priority setting and a number of proposals have remained on the table. Stockholm thus also faces the difficult task of deciding how priorities can be set across the whole of health care.

United Kingdom

Of the five countries under review, the UK is the only one without national guidance on the way priorities might be set. The Department of Health sets health improvement targets (such as the 'Health of the Nation' targets for reductions in mortality and morbidity from particular diseases) for district health authorities (DHAs) and commissioning agencies to aim at, but has not suggested that any specific services should not be funded on the grounds of ineffectiveness or value for money. However, planning guidance for 1994–95 issued by the NHS Executive does go as far as suggesting that purchasers should increasingly base their decisions on evidence of clinical effectiveness. When one regional health authority tried to exclude specific services from funding, it was forced to rescind the decision. The NHS Act calls for a comprehensive service, and that statute, ministers maintain, must be upheld.

Nevertheless, DHAs and commissioning agencies have in practice been free to exclude services if they wish, and some have chosen to drop treatments such as the removal of tattoos and in-vitro fertilization.

Thus, an anomalous situation has arisen with exclusions nominally barred but allowed at district level. This has produced regional disparities which have undermined long-standing efforts to realize uniform provision and has attracted the interest of the Health Select Committee (Ref. 3, paras 112–113).

Clinicians also exercise considerable discretion; some surgeons have refused to perform heart operations on smokers and elderly patients may be denied access to renal dialysis or other expensive treatments[4]. Here, the assessment of outcome is said to be controlling; treatment, the Department of Health maintains, is not denied because of age or lifestyle alone. However, a procedure has yet to be devised to ensure that this is so.

Local discretion has left room for a variety of methods to be employed. Although much interest has been shown in the Oregon experiment and some techniques borrowed from it, no attempt has been made to compile a detailed list. The task is beyond the capacity of individual authorities, and many consider this method too mechanical an approach to priority setting.

Needs assessment

The priority setting process typically begins with an assessment of needs, usually in the form of a broad epidemiological framework, but attempts are being made to establish a closer link with purchasing decisions. The UK is fairly unique in this respect; no similar efforts at assessment are made elsewhere[1].

Budgets, however, are held by an increasing number of GPs who have the right to buy services on their own, thus reducing the primacy of health authority purchasing decisions. Whether GPs hold budgets or not, their referral decisions actually dictate spending patterns. Attempts are being made to link the priorities of health authorities more closely with theirs (Ref. 3, paras 75–79). Only New Zealand, of the other four countries, has offered an arrangement like fundholding, but few doctors, if any, have adopted it.

Cost-effectiveness

With few studies available, little use has been made of data dealing with cost-effectiveness. However, the Department of Health has supported a series of projects to ensure that resources are targeted in a way which achieves the greatest health gain for the population. Much effort is being devoted to the development of clinical guidelines so that the treatment provided is based on sound evidence and is appropriate to the condition at hand. The results are uncertain, and this may have greater effect on the quality than on the cost of care.

Public consultation

Much effort has gone into means of involving the public. Ranking exercises of specific treatments have seldom proved fruitful, perhaps because the public lacks the information and expertise needed to make informed choices.

More promising have been methods to elicit the values which the public believes should guide purchasing decisions. Inspired by the Oregon example, various purchasers have used similar techniques, including questionnaire surveys, opinion polls, focus groups and public meetings.

There is still much uncertainty about how the public's views should be applied. As in Oregon, no clear method has been devised. From surveys that have been made, it would appear that the public wants the medical profession to take primary responsibility, but politicians consider priority setting too important to be left to doctors.

Few changes made

Based on a study of six leading health authorities (including Southampton), priority setting has yet to produce a significant shift in resource allocation[5]. Restrained by calls to keep a 'steady state' during the first two years of the internal market, health authorities made only a modest change in resources. Funding shortages have also restricted room for manoeuvre. As a result, the mentally ill and other so-called 'priority groups' have not realized the gains they were intended to receive from purchasing plans. Indeed, Klein and Redmayne[6] have concluded that the 'political' solution favoured by many authorities is to spread resources around, trying to do a little of everything to keep the pressure groups quiet, rather than making significant changes.

To the extent that reallocations were realized, they have favoured prevention and community care. This applied particularly to authorities faced with the need to reduce expenditure on hospital services. They found it important to sponsor proposals that promised to extend the range of primary care.

Growth money and health gain

The simplest level of priority setting exists for those purchasers who receive growth money. Proposals can be restricted to areas deemed worthy of develop-ment, and funded from the extra money allocated each year from the Exchequer.

One authority (formerly City and Hackney, now part of East London and City) used a two-stage scoring method to judge proposals. In the first stage, bids were ranked on the basis of needs assessment, with the greatest weight being assigned to services which responded to local needs. Then, a short list was prepared and proposals were ranked as follows:

- robustness or the extent to which the proposal can be implemented   0–3
- promotion of equity   0–1
- evidence of effectiveness or cost-effectiveness   0–2
- collaboration or integration with primary care   0–3
- prioritized by the community health council (a statutory organization representing patients)   0–1
- prioritized by local GPs   0–1
- other possible or more appropriate sources of funding   0–5 (negative score)

Thus, the greatest weight was attached to other funding methods, using a negative score as high as five to cancel out the other weightings. The scores were first determined by the Director of Public Health and then discussed by purchasing team managers and members of the health authority. However, this approach is now much harder to sustain, as the purchaser is faced with a real reduction in funding each year and 'growth money' has become a thing of the past.

Empirical development

Priority setting in the UK is thus proceeding in an empirical manner, with decisions and methods left to local determination. Health authority managers would welcome greater involvement by national politicians, and it is widely recognized that priority setting cannot simply be a scientific process, as there are political factors to be considered.

Oregon methods have stimulated interest in priority setting but, elsewhere, no attempt has been made to compile a detailed list covering the whole of health care. Instead, a more modest and cautious approach is being employed.

Issues arising

Difficulties with 'bite-sized chunks'

A promising method was offered by confining the task to 'bite-sized chunks', but this created difficulties of its own. For one thing, there is a tendency, arising only partly from funding problems, to leave choices on the table and not implement them. But this approach also depends on the availability of reliable data so that informed judgements can be made, and that can be obtained more from the acute than the chronic sector.

This can lead to the neglect of services for chronic and vulnerable groups, yet the main aim of priority setting efforts everywhere is to move resources in their direction. Some means must be devised of ensuring needs are met for these groups.

Data deficiencies

Only a minority of health care procedures are backed by reliable evidence of effectiveness, and this makes cost–utility estimates difficult. Judgements have had to be based on the experience of clinicians and whatever costs are available. This leaves only a limited place for the cost–utility, or QALY, approach to priority setting. As Oregon found to its embarrassment, it cannot be applied across the whole of health care.

In Oregon, quality of life considerations were also ruled out because of federal law. How widely this will apply is not clear, but assessments involving quality of life are being increasingly employed elsewhere.

Ethical principles

The need for ethical principles to guide priority setting is generally recognized, and Oregon produced an impressive number. But better methods for applying the principles need to be devised. In Oregon and elsewhere, they are being used in a somewhat arbitrary manner based on the implicit value judgements of those who set priorities.

Public consultation

Priority setting is a controversial subject, and it is generally recognized that the public needs to be consulted before hard choices can be made. Satisfactory methods still need to be devised. The public seems better suited to offer guidance on ethical principles than on choice of specific services.

Need to consult GPs

Where a gatekeeper system exists, GPs or other primary carers make referral decisions and their choices can exert considerable influence on spending patterns. This applies particularly in the UK, where GPs hold budgets of their own and are free to set their own priorities. Better means need to be devised of consulting all GPs and linking their priorities with those of purchasing authorities.

Role of providers

Except in Gavleborg in Sweden, providers have only a limited role in the priority setting process. In the UK, they can present bids for service developments but, otherwise, purchasers tend to make decisions on their own.

But an interest in the development of clinical guidelines is being shown everywhere, and this offers scope for provider involvement. New Zealand is working directly with clinicians to clarify when services should be provided and to whom. This may identify those services which are not cost-effective and enable resources to be shifted in a more beneficial direction.

Linking needs assessment to decisions

Needs assessment can greatly influence priorities, but only in the UK is the process being developed. Better means of assessing needs and relating them to purchasing decisions have to be devised.

These are the main issues arising from international experience and, in the chapter that follows, it will be important to see how they were handled in Southampton.

References

1 Honigsbaum F, Calltorp J, Ham C, Holmstrom S. (1994) *Priority Setting Processes for Healthcare*. Radcliffe Medical Press, Oxford.
2 Honigsbaum F. (1991) *Who Shall Live? Who Shall Die? – Oregon's Health Financing Proposals*. King's Fund College Papers, London.
3 Health Committee (1995) *Priority Setting in the NHS: Purchasing*, Volume I. HMSO, London.
4 Underwood MJ *et al*. (1993) Should smokers be offered coronary by-pass surgery? *British Medical Journal*, **306:** 1047–50.
5 Ham C. (1995) Priority setting in the NHS: reports from six districts. *British Medical Journal*, **307:** 435–8.
6 Klein R, Redmayne S. (1992). *Patterns of Priorities: A Study of the Purchasing and Rationing Policies of Health Authorities*. NAHAT Research Paper No. 7. NAHAT, Birmingham.

2   The Southampton experience

Within the UK, Southampton has been one of the leading authorities developing techniques to set priorities. This section describes the procedures followed since the internal market began in 1991.

Two exercises in priority setting have been carried out: one a simulation, the other for real. The simulation seminar was recorded in a publication of the King's Fund called *Purchasing Dilemmas* and is summarized first[1]. The lessons learned from that exercise, together with the benefit of international experience, have now been applied to the actual process of setting priorities. The way Southampton did it is set out in detail below.

Simulation seminar of 1991

The current exercise was preceded by a simulation seminar held in Southampton in 1991. That was designed to test seven purchasing dilemmas, the most important being the extent to which resources could or should be shifted from interventions dealing with acute care to preventive measures and community services for the chronic sick and priority groups such as the mentally ill.

Three case studies were discussed: two dealt with 'vertical' priorities or the appropriate balance of resources within a programme between prevention, treatment and rehabilitation. The third dealt with 'horizontal' priorities or the extent to which resources could be shifted from one care group to another to achieve an appropriate balance in response to needs.

Case study 1: coronary heart disease

One 'vertical' priority case dealt with coronary heart disease and revealed the difficulty of shifting resources to prevention because of insufficient evidence of effectiveness. Treating the existing 'pool' of disease, in the form of thrombolytic drugs and cardiac artery bypass grafts, had much stronger backing and the government had set targets for health authorities to reach.

Case study 2: acute stroke care

The other 'vertical' priority case dealt with services for elderly people suffering from severe stroke and examined the benefits of, and barriers to, shifting resources from acute to community care. Here, the evidence in favour of either is equivocal and professional opinion might need to be offset against user and carer preference.

Among elderly people and their carers, there is thought to be support for improved community and home services. But information on patient preferences is limited and conflicting views might be found. A shift to community-based care might result in the deaths of more patients with severe strokes, and that raised ethical questions which the public and professionals would want to consider. The case highlighted the importance of testing not only community but GP opinion, since GPs would inevitably bear much of the burden of responsibility for community-based rehabilitation.

This case study thus opened up the possibility of shifting resources from the acute to the rehabilitation stage. Community care changes might accentuate the need since hospital beds could be blocked if social services could not facilitate discharge to nursing homes. Relations between the NHS and other agencies had to be considered more carefully.

More 'heroic' acute intervention would still be required for stroke patients with the best prognosis or with the need for life-saving treatment. That could be determined only after investigation in an acute unit. Also, emphasis might shift back to acute care if more effective treatment emerged.

The study drew attention to the importance of user and carer preferences in addition to evidence of clinical effectiveness.

Case study 3: all care groups

The third case dealt with 'horizontal' priorities or the problem of shifting resources between care groups. The study examined marginal investment proposals using growth money, but recognized that changes at the margin had a cumulative effect on the overall balance of resources between care groups. This had always been the case but had occurred incrementally and largely unseen. It was time to get to grips with the 'big picture'. A sample of managers and clinicians ranked 15 health investment proposals in a survey, with three each divided into five 'care groups' or programmes: health promotion, adult acute, mental health, elderly and children. Decision-makers were not given cost information but were told that any increase in funding for one group could only come at the expense of another.

At the top came treatments for coronary heart disease, childhood accident and breast/cervical cancer. At the bottom came treatment for hernias/varicose veins, services to prevent suicide and bereavement counselling.

If the preferences shown by survey respondents were extrapolated into funding changes by care group, the largest cut (33.75%) would have been made in the health promotion targets of family planning, smoking and HIV/AIDS. The only increase would have been in adult care because of the high rankings given to heart disease and cancer.

All of this ran counter to the authority's objectives of developing community services and protecting the services of 'priority' groups such as the elderly and mentally ill. It illustrated the gulf between expressed (largely rhetorical) priorities and actual decisions and proved to be uncannily prophetic of the real purchasing patterns displayed in subsequent years[2].

Views of experts

This exercise was followed by the presentation of the views of four experts: an epidemiologist, a health economist, a moral philosopher and medical journalist. Two key points emerged.

I A balance must be struck between the rights of individuals to a 'minimum core service' and the need to provide care so that it produces the greatest good for the greatest number of people.

2 Health authorities must give precedence to community need but must decide how that need is to be measured.

The public was not consulted in this exercise, but it was felt that any shifts in the model of care provided (as exemplified in the stroke case) should be made in the light of known consumer preferences. Service restrictions, too, were more likely to be accepted if the process were conducted in an open manner. That raised the problem of how the public should be consulted, a question that was left for further consideration.

Lessons learned

The exercise showed there were no easy answers to resource allocation. It made sense to approach the problem first in the form of 'bite-sized chunks', as in case study I. But even there the evidence available with regard to coronary heart disease was patchy, being much stronger for certain treatments than for prevention. Common sense tells us the latter is the better course to follow but it has not been shown to work sufficiently well.

Case study 2 posed an even greater problem because less evidence was available. Should resources for patients with severe strokes be shifted from acute to community care? Because important ethical questions are involved, priority decisions might have to rely more on the preferences of patients than the judgements of professionals.

But vertical priority setting, difficult as it was, did not pose the formidable challenge of horizontal priorities. How should resources be shifted from one care group to another?

No simple means of comparison are available, and the process inevitably involves subjective judgements. In making these judgements, health authorities had to be clear about the criteria or values they employed and they had to balance four conflicting pressures shown in Figure 2.1.

Before the 1991 reforms, the main pressures came on the vertical axis – from the 'givens' set in the form of fairly prescriptive service targets (e.g. so many heart bypass operations per thousand people)

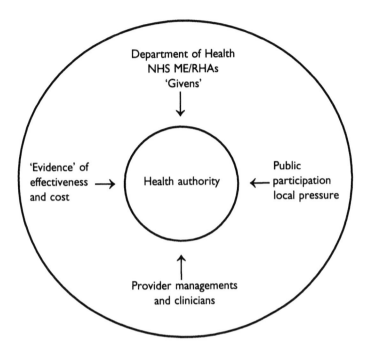

Figure 2.1: Balancing pressures

and from the dialogue with providers. Now, cost-effectiveness data and public participation are likely to play an increasing role. Health authorities were also being pressed to develop a proactive purchaser strategy and not simply react to the demands of providers. By creating a strategic role for purchasers (to secure health gain for the population) the reforms had, perhaps inadvertently, reinvented rational planning to replace the disjointed incrementalism that had come to characterize the NHS.

The growth of commissioning

Before describing the 1994 Purchasing Dilemmas exercise, it is worth reviewing the establishment of the purchasing function and its evolution into commissioning, using Southampton and South West Hampshire Health Commission as an example. This section examines the major factors influencing this developing role.

Development of commissions

Prior to the reforms, district health authorities (DHAs) received a budget from regional health authorities to manage hospital and community services. The services remained under direct district control and the district was charged with staying within the expenditure limits and maintaining the standards of care on offer. Under this system there was little incentive to develop efficient services, and all too often the allocation of resources may have been unduly influenced by those specialists who shouted loudest. Districts were required to generate plans, and these concentrated on the development of services and the capital infrastructure needed to support them.

The 1989 White Paper *Working for Patients* proposed the establishment of purchasing health authorities with a responsibility to assess the health needs of their resident populations and secure services accordingly through the mechanism of market-style contracting with provider hospitals. NHS trusts were to be established in place of directly managed provider units, with increased management freedoms. It was thought that such a market would improve the standards and efficiency of services.

The separation of purchaser and provider roles did not occur immediately across the NHS. Rather, a gradual process of change was initiated which transferred the responsibility for providing services to the unit level of management, leaving the staff at district level free to adopt the purchasing role. These changes involved considerable increase in staff numbers in the personnel and finance functions, which transferred to the units.

The small numbers of staff that remained in districts were responsible for both the management of the remaining units until they became trusts and the development of the purchasing role.

When the reforms were first introduced, there was little widespread awareness of the nature or significance of the purchasing role[3]. Indeed, many DHA general managers moved swiftly to seek appointments as trust chief executives: this was where the 'action' would be. Some thought purchasers would do little more than sign the cheques which enabled providers to function.

Initially the development of the purchaser–provider split appeared to confirm these thoughts. As trusts only emerged slowly, purchasers had to spend significant amounts of time managing the new organization. What development there was revolved around project 26 ('Developing Districts') by the NHS Executive or resulted from simulation exercises[4]. Project 26 attempted to define the functions and, significantly, the East Anglian 'Rubber Windmill' simulations began to explore the dynamics of the internal market – the role of purchasers in securing change and the presence or otherwise of leverage to bring this about[5].

But the purpose of purchasing was perhaps best set out in the Welsh NHS Strategic Intent and Direction (SID) and the 'Local Strategies for Health' initiative arising therefrom[6]. This stated that the purpose of the NHS was to improve people's health and placed a responsibility on purchasers to develop and implement strategies which would secure health gain ('adding years to life and life to years') through a 'people-centred' approach and effective use of resources. Thus, purchasers would have a major *strategic* role in changing the configuration of the services for the local population better to meet their health needs, and this would be achieved through appropriate resource allocation.

In England, rather later, the 1992 White Paper *Health of the Nation* (HON) similarly placed the major strategic focus of the NHS on securing better health[7]. It also identified key areas for health improvement, suggesting the use of targets and identifying effective interventions. This contribution to the strategic direction of purchasing has been widely overlooked, with HON being seen as simply championing health promotion initiatives.

With the realization that resource allocation was available as a tool for achieving strategic change, the problem of priority setting, or indeed rationing, arose. Hence, the first 'Purchasing Dilemmas' simulation in 1991 described above.

Among the many lessons to emerge from this initial foray into the uncomfortable world of priority setting was the potential benefit to be gained for unifying the approach to purchasing primary and secondary care. It made sense that an organization charged with the duty to secure health improvements for the population by allocating resources would benefit from the flexibility and greater scope of controlling resources across the full range of health interventions and the ability to shift resources from less effective to more effective interventions without the encumbrance of structural boundaries.

The former Wessex region established health commissions for this very purpose in 1992. Southampton and South West Hampshire became a health commission in June 1992, merging the functions of the DHA and the Family Health Service Authority (FHSA) (although statutory merger is not facilitated until the anticipated change to primary legislation in April 1996).

Alongside this, HON helped to show how other agencies, when working together, have a significant impact on health. Indeed, health services may have limited impact when considered alongside the socioeconomic determinants of health. In partial recognition of this, and the crucial interrelationships of health and social care provision, the health commission extended its membership to include the assistant director of social services and formed the Southampton and South West Hampshire Health and Social Care Alliance – a network of local agencies whose decisions have an impact on health. It was becoming clear, too, that the commission had a role in influencing and enabling other agencies to bring about change beyond merely 'purchasing' services. Indeed, the development of health services required needs-led strategic involvement which could not be achieved by simply buying 'off the shelf': commissioning was being born.

The development of commissioning in Southampton

The first purchasing plan (1994–99) after the formation of the commission signalled several emerging themes: there was an attempt to consider holistically the whole array of resources available across each sector of health care, a commitment to secure strategic shifts of resources into priority areas and a recognition that more efficient resource allocation demanded a serious look at redeployment within and between programmes, not just spending the marginal sums of 'growth' money sensibly.

This trend was accelerated dramatically in the following year by the development of a local health strategy, looking towards the health of the population in the next century. The health strategy took the HON approach of identifying health improvement targets (for the reduction of mortality or morbidity from specific diseases), but extended their scope to include local major health problems (such as childhood dental disease or unwanted teenage pregnancy) as well as the five 'key areas' of HON. In all, 29 health problems were singled out for attention by the health commission.

The major feature of the health strategy was, however, the adoption of a programme budget approach, linking the amount of disease in the population to the amount expended on it. This decision marked the real transformation into a health commission with a mission of securing better health from being a manager of services (either directly or as an immature purchaser). At last, the purpose (mission) of the commission could be spelled out in specific measurable objectives (health targets) and its performance in managing change linked directly to resource use. Instead of having financial systems measuring contracted activity in terms of services (e.g. specialties), disease-based programme budgeting offered the potential of a rational strategic planning framework for health improvements.

Priority setting and resource allocation

Emerging directly from the work of the health strategy, 'Purchasing Dilemmas 1994' was designed as a decision-making process to determine the relative priorities for resource allocation of a wide range of agreed development options. A total of 49 options were indicated by strategy work as desirable, effective and much needed changes to the current configuration of services purchased. Each would require some investment, either new money or redeployment. The sheer number of options pressing for investment was, however, indicative of the difficulty of getting fine strategic intentions, well supported by thorough evidence, into practice. This remains the major challenge for commissions if they are to prove their worth to the NHS. It is clearly about more than mere money: 'affordability' is always an issue, but Southampton's experience (and the district has been comparatively well off in growth terms) indicates some difficulty in implementing strategies, particularly those involving a significant redeployment of resources either within or across programmes.

The main focus of Purchasing Dilemmas would be to use a marginal analysis approach to prioritizing options for investment within and between eight health programmes. The conference would focus on identifying the criteria applicable to such decisions and seeing whether they could be applied explicitly and rigorously to satisfy the demand for accountable and efficient decision making.

Rational planning and decision making – 1994

Thus, in 1994, Southampton decided to apply the lessons it had learned from the simulation of 1991 to the actual process of decision making. By 1994 the commission was responsible for £234 million of expenditure with only £10 million, or 4% of the total, going to GP fundholders, who covered nearly one-third of the population. Non-cash-limited expenditure for family practitioner services (largely beyond the allocative discretion of the commission) took another £61 million, but that still left £163 million, or 70% of the total, in commission hands.

In the years following the simulation seminar, the commission drew on the methods used in case studies 1 and 2 to develop strategies for change in particular programmes, such as mental health. However, many had remained on the table, and the commission did not have a way to fit these choices into the larger scheme of things. Because of the 'bite-sized chunk' approach of these purchasing strategies, it had never taken a total view. The health strategy had brought these issues to the fore: the time had come to apply 'horizontal' priority setting, drawing on methods employed in case study 3.

Southampton is a capitation gaining district and the commission estimated in its health strategy that it would have growth funds available over the next five years ranging from £22 million (on a low-growth assumption of 1% per year) to £34 million (on a high-growth assumption of 2% per year).

The main issue before the commission was to see whether alterations should be made over time in its basic structure of expenditure with the possibility of disinvestments (meaning withdrawal of funding from some services) in some areas of health care. But that was not its most pressing concern: it also wanted to decide how the growth money at its disposal should be used.

How should growth money be allocated? In many districts, the process begins with inviting bids from providers and compiling a short list for the health authority to consider. Usually, only about 10–15 bids are referred in this way.

Southampton had for some time used a more selective process, identifying the areas in which bids would be welcomed, but on this occasion the commission decided to take a more proactive stance. It wanted to develop its own strategy and not simply respond to the wishes of providers. This was in line with the Department of Health's concern to strengthen the purchasing function.

That was not the only change in the procedure. The non-executive members were keen to play a more active role and wanted to be sure that the criteria used in prioritizing the options were consistent with their aims and values. This meant that no prior short list would be compiled. In addition to those options coming from the strategy review, others had been left on the table from previous years. Some bids also came from providers who sought, for example, £1.3 million more in specialist services. All of this meant that many options would be presented to the commission.

Overview of the Purchasing Dilemmas process

Purchasing Dilemmas 1994 was an event held in the Novotel Hotel, Southampton, on 19 and 20 September 1994. Members of the health commission, aided by expert advisers and in the company of invited observers, considered some 49 options for investment over the next five years. These options were drawn from the work of the health strategy to the year 2000 and a series of individual purchasing strategies and joint commissioning strategies developed over recent months. The 49 options represented those investment decisions over which the commission could exercise its discretion (excluding, for example, prior commitments arising from the current investment programme).

In the weeks preceding the event, a stakeholder consultation had been undertaken. Other agencies, local authorities, GPs, providers and voluntary groups and community interests – represented by the community health council (CHC), parish councils and local sixth form students – were invited to complete a questionnaire about the 49 options. They were asked to rank these quite specific options as high, medium or low priority. The aim of the exercise was to inform the commission of the importance attached to the options by local stakeholders, each of whom had particular knowledge or experience about health services. It was not a 'public' consultation in the full sense of the term.

Simultaneously, staff of the commission had prepared information for members on the costs and benefits of each option. An assessment was made of the attributes of each option in respect of its contribution to the mission and aims of the commission, assuming that these would be the starting point of any criteria used in making decisions.

In order to prepare the commission for the main event, an away day discussion on 6 September 1994 examined some principles of economic analysis and their relevance to resource allocation decisions, together with the particular dilemma of the management of sub-fertility using 'assisted conception' techniques: the 'trial run'.

The objectives of Purchasing Dilemmas are summarized thus:

1 to form a consensus about the relative importance (rank) of a range of potential investments (options):

- decide the criteria
- agree the balance between them
- apply the criteria
- consider the results
- discuss and revise
- pass a ranked list to the investment group for programming

2 to examine the extent to which rationality and explicitness can be brought to bear on this process

3 to involve the whole commission in decision-making on priorities.

In preparation for priority setting, the commission made a 'trial run' with a case study looking at assisted conception.

The process would proceed as follows.

1 Strategies had been developed covering 29 health problems divided between eight health programmes.

2 Forty-nine options were selected as potential contributors to health gain.

3 GPs and other stakeholders assessed the 49 options in terms of their benefit or importance.

4 The commission developed criteria with the aid of experts, who presented their views in a 'fishbowl' discussion before the commission.

5 The commission determined the relative importance of criteria by assigning weights to each.

6 The commission ranked the 49 options based on the criteria they had developed. Rankings based on cost were conducted separately because the commission was unclear about how much this should influence their decisions. Another ranking was conducted within one health programme to produce a clearer view of the criteria employed.

7 The commission found the need to consider additional criteria and rank all the options programme by programme.

8 An investment programme (part of the purchasing plan) was produced after approval of the final rankings.

Some consideration was given to whether funds spent on existing services could be freed through disinvestments. Targeting specific 'less effective' treatment was thought to be impractical, and a health economist proposed the pursuit of efficiency savings instead. (See Chapter 4 for a fuller discussion.)

The result was as follows: implementation was to proceed over a five-year period with 18 options funded in year one, seven in year two, one in year three, three in year four and one in year five. Nineteen were not included.

The 25 interventions scheduled in the first two years stand the best chance of being implemented. It all depends on the funds ultimately available and the risk of other, more pressing, claims on available funds arising in later years.

The final rankings agreed by the commission could not be simply transplanted into the purchasing plan either, as pragmatic programming considerations (such as phasing and the need to keep each year of the plan in financial balance) came into play.

Six options ranked in the first 20 were not due to be implemented in the first two years; their place was taken by others ranked lower on the list due to such considerations.

Trial run

Before the main 'Purchasing Dilemmas' event, it was decided to have a trial run so that the commission could see how its own criteria might be developed. The session started with an introduction to the basic principles of health economics and then went on to consider a specific case study. Assisted conception was the problem chosen. It was one of the more common procedures excluded by health authorities and would provide an opportunity to understand what criteria were relevant to such a decision.

Southampton had long offered tubal surgery, but it had rejected *in-vitro* fertilization (IVF) in 1986 when the procedure had a lower success rate. At that time, patients could be transferred elsewhere for treatment but, with the 1991 reforms, it could be done only exceptionally as an extracontractual referral with costs borne by the commission. That put responsibility in the hands of the public health director, and he found decisions hard to make without an explicit steer from the commission. This exercise would give the commission an opportunity to apply its own judgement since it was ultimately responsible for the expenditure incurred.

During the discussion, two conflicting criteria emerged: cost-effectiveness and equity. Though more cost-effective than tubal surgery, IVF had a low success rate and each cycle was expensive to perform. On the other hand, infertility caused much distress and could result in emotional disability. If money could be spent on abortion, it was argued, why not infertility?

The issue proved difficult to resolve since few data were available on current costs or the effectiveness of the infertility services that providers offered. The discussion then centred on this question: Is infertility a health or social problem? If the latter, some members felt it could be excluded. This was finally settled when it was suggested that consideration might be given to any condition that the Health Service could do something about regardless of theoretical and flawed definitions of 'health' as opposed to 'social' problems. However, it was noted that other districts had restricted access and made only limited sums available for IVF.

The session ended with the agreement that IVF was a relevant issue but its relative priority would be deferred until all 49 options were considered.

Development of the health strategy

As discussed earlier, the process had started with the development of the health strategy during 1993. Health care expenditure was grouped into eight disease-based programmes: injury, mental health, cancer, circulatory diseases, mobility and the senses, infection and internal diseases, pregnancy and the newborn, other health programmes (not disease-specific).

From these, the public health directorate had identified 29 health problems that were either a major cause of mortality and morbidity in terms of the number of people affected or a relatively large local health problem. Prominent among the former were heart disease, various cancers, stroke and mental illness, while child dental health and teenage pregnancy had caused much local concern. For the most part, the first group conformed with national and regional priorities since Southampton's population profile is similar to the national picture. For an overview of the health problems, see Appendix A.

For each of the 29 problems, the commission then assessed their impact in terms of mortality, morbidity and cost. This was followed by the selection of interventions which would reduce the risk or impact of the problem, using assessments of effectiveness and value for money.

For example, in the programme of injury, the commission had focused on accidents and poisoning. Where accidents were concerned, risk could be reduced by the use of safety devices which were found to be effective and to be good value for money. Similarly, the impact of accidents could be reduced by immediate care which was effective and moderate value for money.

Targets were then set for each health problem with the selection of programme changes best designed to meet them. For example, to reduce the risk of accidents, eight interventions had been considered, and from these three programme changes were proposed. Similarly, to reduce the impact of accidents, six interventions had been considered and from these five program-me changes were proposed. There were thus eight programme changes (or 'options') from the injury programme for the commission to consider.

From the eight health programmes, a total of 49 options emerged as listed in Appendix B with their indicative costs.

Criteria used in health strategy

Up to this point, the process had been conducted within the commission using three essential criteria: local need, effectiveness and value for money. Consideration was also given to the extent to which programme changes were relevant to the commission's past commitments and strategic direction.

In view of funding uncertainties, high (2% per year) and low (1% per year) growth figures were estimated. Proportions between health programmes were changed on the basis of four assessments:

1 the relative priorities of each programme

2 the distance from health targets

3 the availability of effective interventions

4 the efficiency of current resource use.

The formula shared out the available growth by applying a weighting factor to the current share of expenditure thus:

- injury – 0.80

- mental health – 1.36

- cancer – 0.80

- circulatory diseases – 1.20

- mobility and the senses – 1.04

- infection and internal diseases – 1.04

- pregnancy and the newborn – 0.88

- other health programmes – 0.88.

Mental health was intended to benefit most. Its share of resources was to increase from 13.7% to about 15%, with the largest share of growth money being devoted to developments in this programme.

Table 2.1 shows an extract from the health strategy showing how formula shares were derived from the factors mentioned above and applied to growth forecasts to produce target investment patterns

Table 2.1 Health strategy to the year 2000 – programme changes

Health programme	Share (%)			Programme changes (£ millions)					
	Current 1993–94	Target 1999-2000		Low growth			High growth		
		Low growth	High growth	Available total	Planned investment	Balance	Available total	Planned investment	Balance
Injury	6.1	6.2	6.2	1.3	0.3	1.0	1.8	0.3	1.5
Mental health	13.7	14.8	15.0	4.4	3.4	1.0	6.5	3.4	3.1
Cancer	5.0	5.2	5.1	1.0	0.3	0.7	1.5	0.3	1.2
Circulatory disease	8.8	9.3	9.7	2.4	0.3	2.1	4.6	0.3	4.3
Mobility and the senses	18.4	19.2	19.2	4.4	0.3	4.1	6.6	0.3	6.3
Infection and internal disease	24.4	25.6	25.5	5.7	0.4	5.3	8.7	0.4	8.3
Pregnancy and the newborn	5.3	5.4	5.4	1.1	0.3	0.8	1.7	0.3	1.4
Other health programmes	8.3	8.6	8.5	1.7	0.4	1.3	2.6	0.4	2.2
Unassigned	8.1	4.2	3.9	–	–	–	–	–	–
Commissioning organization	1.9	1.5*	1.5*	–	–	–	–	–	–
Total	100.0	100.0	100.0	22.0	5.7	16.3	34.0	5.7	28.3

*Target commissioning organization overhead from 1995–96.

over the next five years. Planned investments (i.e. those identified in the current investment programme) are set against the sums available, leaving a balance available for additional programme changes.

Information presented to the commission members for Purchasing Dilemmas

In selecting the 49 options, health benefit had been the main criterion. Equity, choice and other criteria had not been prime factors. However, before they were presented to the commission, assessments were made of the extent to which the options contributed to equity, choice, personal responsibility and access (in regard to both waiting time and local provision). A maximum score of one was assigned for each attribute based on the informed judgements of commission staff.

For example, here is the score assigned to home-based palliative care:

health benefit	I
improved equity	0
increased choice	I
encouraging personal responsibility	0
improved access to waiting list	0
improved access to local care	I
Total	3

Cost–utility data were lacking for more precise evaluation. Of the 49 changes, only ten were found to have QALY data associated with them, as shown in Appendix C. The commission had to use whatever cost information was available to assist in the ranking process, including the bids supplied by providers.

The main aim of the process was to assess potential for benefit to the population as a whole. This sought to take account of life expectancy and/or quality of life without having specific measures available. For the health benefit scores assigned to each option, see Appendix D. For the assessments of other criteria, see Appendix E.

The commission was also presented with the share of current resources allocated to each of the eight health programmes and shown how these proportions might change over a five-year period (as described above).

Stakeholder consultation

To aid the planning process, the commission had formed a Health and Social Care Alliance which included GPs (fundholders as well as non-fundholders), the community health council, social services, education, local authority environmental health, housing and leisure, secondary care providers (including Southampton University Hospitals Trust and Southampton Community Health Services Trust) and the independent and voluntary sector.

No attempt was made to consult the general public as part of this particular exercise, but the alliance did contain groups representative of public opinion. The aim was to seek the views of the commission's partners in health care and social care on which options represented the greatest benefits.

Earlier, between December 1993 and February 1994, the alliance partners had supplied views, information and ideas for the health strategy.

An attempt had been made to obtain some sense of the values held by the community. This was done by means of case vignettes (for example, one concern-ed the pros and cons of expensive drug treatment for depression) so as to reveal more clearly the way preferences were made and the trade-offs between them.

A concern for equity and a fair allocation of resources was apparent, along with a call for a locality approach to needs assessment. Also, more effective links between GPs and social services were felt to be crucial.

Though some consultation was seen as desirable, the main message coming from the stakeholders was that they wanted the commissioners to make the hard decisions. It was felt that the subject was too complex for general consideration; that the public did not have the information needed to make careful evaluations of clinical benefit and cost-effectiveness.

Questionnaire survey

However, stakeholders were given the opportunity to apply their own rankings to the 49 options presented in a questionnaire survey. Because of the short timescale allowed in the planning process (and its overlap with the summer holiday period), only 72 responses were received of the 375 questionnaires sent out, and 34 came from GPs.

With so many options, respondents undoubtedly found the ranking process difficult and probably felt that more information was needed about outcome, cost and the number of people affected by each service.

Stakeholders were asked to assign priorities within the eight health programmes, using a score for each option of three for high, two for medium and one for low. The results of the exercise were fully reported at the Purchasing Dilemmas exercise and are summarized in Appendix F.

The highest scores went to the options dealing with cancer and circulatory diseases, the lowest to injury and infection/internal disease.

GP rankings

The responses from GPs were of particular importance because of the influence they exert on commission spending.

Because the replies from GPs represented nearly half the total received from stakeholders, their rankings did much to determine rankings as a whole. They assigned the highest priority to waiting times for elective surgery and the lowest to information for accident prevention.

Allocation of funds by health programme

Stakeholders were also given the chance to suggest *changes* in the way funds were distributed across health programmes. Of the 43 who disagreed with the current allocation, more money on average went to the cancer and circulatory disease programmes, while slightly less went to infection and internal disease and mobility and the senses. However, where the allocation of additional funds was concerned, the priority differed. All 72 responded to this question and the mental health programme received the highest percentage.

Criteria employed

What did these findings suggest about the criteria stakeholders used and how would they conform with those to be employed by the commission? In the view of commission staff, four themes stood out: waiting time, local access, choice and health benefit. Less importance was attached to personal responsibility. The two exercises held earlier (in December and February) also revealed a pronounced concern for equity not simply in terms of local access (of special importance to those living in rural areas), but for the fair allocation of resources between different socioeconomic groups and ethnic minorities.

However, with only 72 responses, not much weight could be attached to the statistics of the consultation as a whole. In any future consultation, it was clear that more time should be allowed. Forty-nine options were clearly too many for stakeholders to handle with ease and, while more information would have arguably helped, it might merely have made the task even harder.

Identifying criteria

With the arrival of 19 September 1994, the first day of the exercise, the commission now had to decide how it would rank the 49 options. The next stage called for fuller development of its own criteria than had been possible in the trial run.

Aims contained in the mission statement of the commission, set out in its health strategy, provided a starting point for criteria to use. These were as follows: equity, health gain, value for money, care closer to home, choice and personal responsibility.

Discussion centred on the six criteria derived from the mission statement, and the main issue revolved around the value of health gain as opposed to equity. Setting priorities according to health gain and value for money would ensure that the commission made best use of the limited resources available. But equity was also important to consider, so that services were extended to groups that were hard to reach and where there was a considerable burden of disease, such as ethnic minorities and the homeless.

Health gain, it was argued, could be considered from the population or individual point of view. The commission would stress the former while clinicians and their patients would be concerned with the latter. It was noted that another health authority had spent £500 000 to treat one individual and this could restrict the provision of other services that might contribute more to health gain.

Conflicting views were expressed about the value of choice. On the one hand, it was argued that choice conflicts with value for money in that it entails the duplication of services. Others felt that it could have the opposite effect where, for example, home delivery was offered in the case of pregnancy. Health gain could also be promoted if patients were given more information so that, with the aid of doctors, they chose care appropriate to their circumstances.

It was apparent from the discussion that differences existed over the meaning of the words used to describe the six criteria. Health gain, equity, choice, access and personal responsibility had to be defined in clearer terms.

Views of experts

To help the commission decide what criteria to employ and how to define them, seven experts then presented their views on priority setting in a fishbowl discussion held before members. The experts consisted of a neurosurgeon, a psychogeriatrician, a GP, two health economists, a medical ethicist and a director of community service. (See Appendix G for biographical profiles of each and Chapter 4 for statements of their views.)

Again, the main issue revolved around the value of health gain as opposed to equity. One of the health economists stressed a utilitarian approach to priority setting so that the array of health services provided had the effect of producing the greatest good for the greatest number of people. The medical ethicist, on the other hand, stressed the principle of equity and the right of each individual to obtain the care needed. However, he did allow for restrictions on access dependent on clinician assessment of potential clinical benefit or funding considerations.

The neurosurgeon found the commission's task formidable and recognized the validity of its role in setting priorities. The GP urged bold action; if mistakes were made, they could be corrected later. Only a body at the level of the commission with its access to relevant information and public health advice, he felt, could pursue policies that would totally reshape a service and it should concentrate efforts in this area, perhaps leaving more minor or marginal changes to smaller purchasers such as GPs.

The director of community service urged the commission to be open about the criteria it employed, and not rely on 'gut feel', which could mean 'prejudice'. Her concern, like that of public stakeholders, lay in favour of equity. She feared that a stress on utility might mean further disadvantage for minority groups.

The psychogeriatrician also tended to favour equity, but with his main concern focused on the needs of the chronic sick as opposed to those in the acute sector. In particular, he did not want to see a high priority assigned to the costly option designed to reduce waiting times for elective surgery. That would absorb £1 900 000 of growth money and sharply reduce the amount available for the chronic sick.

Once again, differences arose over the meaning of the words used to describe the criteria. In particular, clearer definitions were needed of health gain and equity. Health gain had to be linked with costs and the number of people who would benefit. For more informed choices to be made, these data ought to be shown for each of the 49 interventions, but only limited information was available.

Determining importance of criteria

The time had come to rank the 49 options, but before the commission could do so, it had to determine what criteria to use and what weights to assign to each. Some consideration was given to links with other agencies and implementation problems, as well as to the national priorities set out in planning guidance. It was decided to leave these considerations to later and provide rankings that would show the commission's own priorities without regard to external pressure.

Unsure of how to assess value for money, the commission decided to put costs aside for the moment and assign weights to the other five benefit criteria in its mission statement. To make this assessment, one of the health economists suggested that 100 points be spread across the five criteria in order to allow greater scope for scoring. Each of the 12 members of the commission assigned scores and the results are shown in Table 2.2.

Health gain was clearly the criterion to which all but two members attached the most importance. Equity came next; only one member put equity below one of the remaining three criteria.

Here are the averages of the weights assigned:

health gain	0.42
equity	0.25
local access	0.13
personal responsibility	0.12
choice	0.11

Health gain had the highest ranking, but equity came next and this conformed with the importance assigned to this value by stakeholders, particularly those representing the community.

Table 2.2 Commission members' scores for benefit criteria

Health gain	Equity	Choice	Personal responsibility	Access to local care
50	20	10	5	15
28	18	18	18	18
25	35	10	10	10
24	26	23	13	14
50	20	10	5	15
35	25	10	15	15
50	20	5	15	10
30	30	10	10	20
40	10	10	20	10
40	20	10	20	10
40	20	10	10	20
40	40	10	5	5

Preliminary ranking of 49 options

Using these weighted criteria and the scores assigned to each of the 49 options earlier (Appendices D and E), commission staff then made two rankings of the 49 interventions – one based on the five benefit criteria alone, the other bringing in the cost data that were available. The results are shown in Table 2.3.

An attempt was then made to glean a clearer sense of the criteria held by members to be important by relating them to the ranking of specific options. This procedure was suggested by the convenor of the session, Professor Chris Ham. By forcing participants to make choices and then debating why the choices were made, it was possible to identify the values employed.

Table 2.3 Results of first ranking

	First ranking: total weighted benefits			First ranking: benefits per pound	
Rank	Option no.	Description	Rank	Option no.	Description
1	8.1	Communication service	1	3.2	Specialist cancer teams
2	7.2	Sex education/contraception clinics	2	2.4	Brief interventions
3	2.6	Information/support to carers	3	2.6	Information/support to carers
4	5.6	Equipment/aids	4	7.4	Folic acid
5	2.1	Community mental health teams	5	4.3	Targeted stroke prevention
6	3.1	Palliative care (home based)	6	6.4	Parent/carer oral health
7	1.5	Multiagency accident prevention	7	6.5	Targeted oral hygiene
8	2.9	Counselling in primary care	8	8.2	Child protection training
9	7.4	Folic acid	9	6.1	Asthma patient education
10	3.2	Specialist cancer teams	10	8.4	Smoking advice
11	1.7	Safety aids	11	1.3	Community first aid
12	4.3	Targeted stroke prevention	12	1.5	Multiagency prevention
13	6.4	Parent/carer oral health	13	2.8	Detection/treatment depression
14	6.5	Targeted oral hygiene	14	8.3	Child protection assessment
15	4.1	Cardiac rehabilitation	15	5.5	Preadmission clinics
16	4.2	Stroke rehabilitation	16	8.6	Communication services
17	8.7	Domiciliary care	17	7.2	Sex education/contraceptive clinics
18	2.7	Respite care (mental health)	18	3.1	Palliative care
19	2.10	Supported housing	19	6.2	Sex education
20	2.8	Detection/treatment depression	20	7.5	Paramedic obstetrics
21	5.7	Mobile retinopathy	21	6.3	Community needle exchange
22	8.2	Child protection training	22	1.7	Safety aids
23	8.3	Child protection assessment	23	4.1	Cardiac rehabilitation
24	1.4	Accident and emergency	24	8.5	Dietetics training

Table 2.3, *continued*

	First ranking: total weighted benefits			First ranking: benefits per pound	
Rank	Option no.	Description	Rank	Option no.	Description
25	2.3	Home/day detoxification	25	3.4	Skin lesions recognition
26	2.4	Brief interventions	26	5.7	Retinopathy screening
27	6.1	Asthma education	27	1.2	Immediate care
28	6.2	Sex education	28	1.6	Prevention information (accidents)
29	8.4	Smoking advice	29	2.5	Substance misuse education
30	5.2	Community orthopaedics	30	3.3	Skin cancer prevention
31	5.4	Community rehabilitation (orthopaedic)	31	8.7	Domiciliary care
32	7.3	Assisted conception	32	5.6	Equipment aids
33	7.5	Paramedic obstetrics	33	2.3	Home/day detoxification
34	3.4	Skin lesions recognition	34	5.2	Community orthopaedics
35	6.3	Needle exchange	35	1.4	Accident and emergency
36	8.1	Waiting times	36	1.8	Trauma centres
37	1.3	Community first aid	37	7.1	New maternity care
38	2.5	Substance misuse education	38	4.2	Stroke rehabilitation
39	3.3	Skin cancer prevention	39	2.7	Respite care
40	8.5	Dietetics	40	2.9	Counselling in primary care
41	7.1	New maternity care	41	5.4	Community rehabilitation (orthopaedic)
42	2.2	Locally based hospital units (LBHUs)	42	2.1	Community mental health teams
43	1.2	Immediate care	43	7.3	Assisted conception
44	1.6	Prevention information (accidents)	44	2.10	Supported housing
45	1.8	Trauma centres	45	2.2	LBHUs
46	1.1	Mixed ambulance trials	46	8.1	Waiting times

Table 2.3, *continued*

		First ranking: total weighted benefits			First ranking: benefits per pound
Rank	Option no.	Description	Rank	Option no.	Description
47	5.5	Readmission clinics – not ranked	47	1.1	Mixed crews
48	5.1	Care attendants – not ranked	48	5.1	Care attendants – not ranked
49	5.3	Knee replacements – not ranked	49	5.3	Knee replacements – not ranked

The five maternity options were chosen for this purpose with the results shown in Table 2.4.

Table 2.4 Revised rankings – maternity and the newborn

		Overall rankings by	
	Rank by discussion	Five criteria (total benefit)	Plus cost (benefit per pound)
Education and contraception	First	2 (first)	17 (third)
New models	Second	41 (fifth)	37 (fourth)
Paramedic	Third	33 (fourth)	20 (second)
Folic acid	Fourth	9 (second)	4 (first)
Assisted conception	Fifth	32 (third)	43 (fifth)

The first two options were the clear top choices. It was difficult to correlate these rankings with the explicit criteria used earlier, and implicit value judgements were again felt to be more important. This may explain why new models of care came second despite the fact that the criterion with the largest weighting, health gain, was not considered to be one of its strengths.

The top ranking given to education and contraception owed much to concern about teenage pregnancy in Southampton. Needs assessment thus exerted considerable influence on this choice.

Ranking of the options

A comparison of the two methods used to rank the 49 options showed sharp differences. One had been based on the five criteria which had weights assigned to them; the other incorporated the cost data available. Using the five criteria, community mental health teams had come fifth, but when the programme's substantial costs were considered it fell to 42. Advice to reduce smoking was ranked at 29 when the five criteria were used, but it rose to ten because of the small costs involved.

Sharp differences also applied to the options in the one health programme that had been ranked by discussion – maternity. Most noticeably, new models of maternity care came second when ranked by discussion but fell close to the bottom in the two overall rankings.

Startled by these differences, the commission decided to abandon any
further attempt to rank the 49 options as a whole. It was more
manageable to rank the few options in each health programme and then
assign overall rankings based on the formula shares assigned to
programmes in the health strategy document (*see* pages 32–4).

The commission also felt the need to consider more than the five
criteria it had initially employed. Other criteria had clearly
influenced the rankings in the maternity example. So, a discussion
on the second day of the exercise produced the following additional
criteria:

- *number* of people who would benefit

- *severity* of the condition

- *ease of implementation*: Is there a worked-up purchasing strategy
  to give robustness to the proposal?

- *jurisdiction/control*: Is it within the sole control of the commission
  or is it dependent on the commitment of other agencies such as
  social services? This conflicted to some extent with. . .

- *alliance links* (the importance of joint working with other
  agencies)

- *continuity* with current purchasing shifts

- *strategic impact* (the scale of the change)

- *stakeholder expectations*

- *givens*, i.e. national and regional policy initiatives.

The last of these was felt to be the single most compelling criterion,
which did not create a problem if it was consistent with local
priorities, but may give rise to serious moral dilemmas if it conflicted
with them. These 'second-order criteria' would, in effect, modify the
priorities resulting from applying the 'mission statement' criteria in
their pure form.

With these considerations in mind, the commission proceeded to
discuss and assign rankings to the options within each health
programme in turn. Since the maternity options had been ranked
earlier, only the seven remaining programmes had to be ranked.

These results were then presented back to the commission at its regular public meeting the following day for final approval (Table 2.5).

Table 2.5 Ranking within programme area judged by the health commission, 20 September 1994

	Total score	Average score out of 10	Ranking
Injury			
Trauma centre	38	2.9	1
Accident and emergency	40	3.1	2
Multiagency prevention	48	3.7	3
Mixed crew trials	52	4.0	4
Community first aid	73	5.4	5
Prevention information	72	5.5	6
Immediate care	73	5.6	7
Safety aids	75	5.8	8
Mental health			
Community teams	20	1.5	1
Respite care	52	4.0	2
Substance misuse education	68	5.2	3
Counselling	68	5.2	3
Information/support to carers	71	5.5	5
Supported housing	77	5.9	6
Home and day detoxification	81	6.2	7
LBHUs	91	7.0	8
Brief intervention	94	7.2	9
Detection and treatment of depression	93	7.2	9
Cancer			
Specialist teams	20	1.5	1
Home-based palliative care	24	1.8	2
Skin cancer prevention	41	3.2	3
Early skin cancer	45	3.5	4
Circulatory disease			
Stroke rehabilitation	21	1.6	1
Cardiac rehabilitation	27	2.1	2
Targeted stroke prevention	30	2.3	3

Continued

Table 2.5, *continued*

	Total score	Average score out of 10	Ranking
Mobility and the senses			
Equipment aids	34	2.6	1
Community rehabilitation	46	3.5	2
Retinopathy screening	46	3.5	2
Community orthopaedic clinic	51	3.9	4
Knee replacements	53	4.1	5
Care attendants	54	4.2	6
Preadmission clinics	79	6.1	7
Infection and internal disease			
Sex education	22	1.7	1
Asthma education	31	2.4	2
Needle exchange	38	2.9	3
Parent oral health	48	3.7	4
Targeted oral hygiene	55	4.2	5
Maternity and the newborn			
Education and contraception			1
New models of care			2
Paramedic obstetrics			3
Folic acid			4
Assisted conception			5
Other			
Waiting list	24	1.8	1
Domiciliary care	38	2.9	2
Child protection training	52	4.0	3
Child protection assessment	55	4.2	4
Smoking advice	54	4.2	4
Communication service	55	4.2	4
Dietetics	66	6.6	7

Purchasing plan

The final stages of the process involved incorporation of the prioritized options into the investment programme of the commission's five-year purchasing plan. As this had been planned on a high growth assumption of 2%, it was possible to accommodate 30 of the 49 over the five-year plan. However, if available resources do not match the assumption, the programme will have to be trimmed. Similarly, those options programmed towards the end of the strategic period are at most risk of displacement by other priorities as they arise during the next five years.

The process by which the ranked options were incorporated into the programme was as follows:

1 Available resources, starting with the first year of the plan, were apportioned across the eight health programmes according to the formula shares set out in the health strategy.

injury	0.80
mental health	1.36
circulatory diseases	1.20
mobility and the senses	1.04
infection and internal disease	0.88
other health programmes	0.88

2 Options were incorporated into the programme in rank order as far as possible.

The order in which options would be implemented could not always follow the order in which they were ranked. Account had to be taken of other factors such as previous commitments, continuity of phased investment, and the need for each year of the Investment Programme to be in balance with expected available resources. The table below shows the final results with the score assigned to each option and the year in which it would be implemented.

Table 2.6 Outcome of rankings in purchasing plan (investment programme)

Option in ranked order		Implemented in
2.1	Community teams	Year 1
8.1	Waiting list	Year 1
1.8	Trauma centres	Not specified
1.4	Accident and emergency	Year 1
3.2	Specialist teams	Year 1
7.2	Education and contraception	Year 1
6.2	Sex education	Year 1
8.7	Domiciliary care	Year 1

Continued

Table 2.6, *continued*

Option in ranked order		Implemented in
1.5	Multiagency prevention	Year 2
3.1	Home-based palliative care	Year 1
5.6	Equipment aids	Year 1
1.1	Mixed crew trials	Year 1
7.1	New models of care	Year 2
6.1	Asthma education	Not specified
8.2	Child protection training	Year 2
8.4	Smoking advice	Not specified
5.4	Community rehabilitation	Year 4
5.7	Retinopathy screening	Year 4
8.3	Child protection assessment	Year 2
8.6	Communication service	Not specified
1.3	Community first aid	Not specified
2.7	Respite care	Year 1
1.6	Prevention information	Not specified
7.5	Paramedic obstetrics	Year 1
1.2	Immediate care	Not specified
7.4	Folic acid	Year 2
1.7	Safety aids	Not specified
5.2	Community orthopaedic clinics	Year 5
5.3	Knee replacements	Not specified
6.3	Needle exchange	Not specified
5.1	Care attendants	Not specified
3.3	Skin cancer prevention	Not specified
4.2	Stroke rehabilitation	Year 1
3.4	Early skin cancer recognition	Not specified
2.5	Substance misuse education	Year 1
2.9	Counselling	Year 2
2.6	Information/support to carers	Year 1
7.3	Assisted conception	Not specified
6.4	Oral health education	Not specified
2.10	Supported housing	Year 1
4.1	Cardiac rehabilitation	Year 1
8.5	Dietetics	Not specified
2.3	Home and day detoxification	Year 3
6.5	Targeted oral hygiene	Not specified
5.5	Preadmission clinics	Not included
4.3	Targeted stroke prevention	Year 1
2.8	Detection and treatment of depression	Year 2

Continued

Table 2.6, *continued*

Option in ranked order		Implemented in
2.4	Brief intervention	Not included

Notes: 1 'Not specified' refers to options which were not specifically listed in the published purchasing plan, although working documents included them for consideration post year 3.
2 'Not included' means not included in the plan, even in working papers.
3 The investment programme is structured by health programme. These options have been rearranged into a single list by applying the formula shares weighting factor in order to enable comparisons to be made with the other overall rankings.

If grouped by year of implementation, the total number of options for each year is as follows:

Year	Total
1	18
2	7
3	1
4	3
5	1
No action	19
	49

The high-priority options are not spread evenly by the health programme. This can be seen from Table 2.7.

Table 2.7 Twenty-five options to be implemented in years 1 and 2 by health programme (rank in parentheses following option)

Injury	Mental health	Cancer	Circulatory disease	Mobility	Infection	Pregnancy	Other
1.4 (4)	2.1 (1)	3.2 (5)	4.2 (33)	5.6 (11)	6.2 (7)	7.2 (6)	8.1 (2)
1.5 (9)	2.7 (22)	3.1 (10)	4.1 (41)			7.1 (13)	8.7 (8)
1.1 (12)	2.5 (35)		4.3 (46)			7.5 (24)	8.2 (15)
	2.9 (36)					7.4 (26)	8.3 (19)
	2.6 (37)						
	2.10 (40)						
	2.8 (48)						

Rankings compared

How do these overall rankings compare with the two made earlier, one based on the five weighted criteria and the other with costs incorporated? The effect can be shown by confining the comparison to the conditions given the highest rank (in the top 20) and those to be implemented in the first two years (Table 2.8).

Table 2.8 Comparison of purchasing plan with earlier rankings

Option		Purchasing plan	Total weighted benefit	Benefit per pound
2.1	Community teams	I	5	42
8.1	Waiting list	2	36	46
1.8	Trauma centres	3 (not specified)	45	36
1.4	Accident and emergency	4	24	35
3.2	Specialist teams	5	10	I
7.2	Education and contraception	6	2	17
6.2	Sex education	7	28	19
8.7	Domiciliary care	8	17	31
1.5	Multiagency prevention	9	7	12
3.1	Palliative care	10	6	18
5.6	Equipment aids	11	4	32
1.1	Mixed crew trials	12	47	47
7.1	New models of care	13	41	37
6.1	Asthma education	14 (not specified)	27	9
8.2	Child protection	15	22	8
8.4	Smoking advice	16 (not specified)	29	10
5.4	Community rehabilitation	17 (year 4)	31	41
5.7	Retinopathy screening	18 (year 4)	21	26
8.3	Child protection assessment	19	23	14
8.6	Community service	20 (not specified)	I	16
2.7	Respite care	22 (year 1)	18	39
7.5	Paramedic obstetrics	24 (year 1)	33	20
7.4	Folic acid	26 (year 2)	9	4
4.2	Stroke rehabilitation	33 (year 1)	16	38
2.5	Substance misuse education	35 (year 1)	38	29
2.9	Counselling	36 (year 2)	8	40
2.6	Information/support to carers	37 (year 1)	3	3
2.10	Support housing	40 (year 1)	19	44

Continued

Table 2.8, *continued*

Option		Purchasing plan	Total weighted benefit	Benefit per pound
4.1	Cardiac rehabilitation	41 (year 1)	15	23
4.3	Targeted stroke prevention	46 (year 1)	12	5
2.8	Detection and treatment of depression	48 (year 2)	20	13

This comparison indicates a radical change in commission priorities when it came to the final rankings. Nearly half the options with the highest priority – 14 out of 31 – had much lower rankings (above number 20) on the basis of the five weighted criteria.

This was most noticeable with regard to waiting lists and accident and emergency, which were given much higher rankings owing to national priorities emanating from the Patient's Charter and government initiatives. National priorities were also responsible for the higher rankings given to the options dealing with child protection and substance misuse.

Health gain was the criterion given the most weight, and what this comparison suggests is that it did tend to dominate thinking at first. But other factors had to be considered before an investment programme could be finalized. At that point national priorities and previous strategic commitments assumed greater importance.

Equity was the criterion given the second highest weight at first, and its influence can be seen in the programme finally approved.

Comparison with GP rankings

How do the commission's final rankings compare with those made by GPs? Their rankings represented nearly half (34 of 72) of those received from stakeholders (Table 2.9).

This comparison reveals a close correlation between GP and commission priorities. The top 15 on the GP's list will be implemented in years one and two, and so will 17 of the top 20. For various pressing reasons, numbers 5, 7–9, 11, 12, 15 and 20 on the GP's list will all be

Table 2.9 Comparison of GP rankings and commission rankings

Option no.		GP ranking	Commission ranking	Implement-ation year
8.1	Waiting lists	1	2	1
1.8	Trauma centres	2	3	–
2.1	Community teams	3 =	1	1
3.1	Home-based palliative care	3 =	10	1
4.2	Stroke rehabilitation	5 =	33	1
7.2	Education/contraception	5 =	6	1
2.7	Respite/day care	7 =	22	1
5.1	Care attendants	7 =	31	–
2.6	Information/support to carers	9 =	37	1
3.2	Cancer specialist teams	9 =	5	1
4.1	Cardiac rehabilitation	11	41	1
2.9	Counselling	12	36	2
6.2	Sex education	13	7	1
1.1	Mixed crew trials	14	12	1
2.5	Substance misuse education	15 =	35	1
5.4	Community rehabilitation	15 =	17	4
8.7	Domiciliary care	15 =	8	1
6.1	Asthma education	18 =	14	–
8.3	Child protection assessment	18 =	19	2
5.5	Preadmission clinics	20	45	–
1.3	Community first aid	21 =	21	–
2.3	Home/day detoxification	21 =	43	3
5.3	Knee replacements	21 =	29	–
5.2	Community orthopaedic	24	28	5
7.5	Paramedic obstetrics	25	24	1
7.4	Folic acid	26	26	1
1.4	Accident and emergency	27	4	1
2.10	Supported housing	28 =	40	1
5.6	Equipment/aids	28 =	11	1
5.7	Mobile retinopathy screening	28 =	18	4
7.1	New maternity care	28 =	13	1
8.4	Smoking advice	28 =	16	–
8.2	Child protection training	33 =	15	2

Continued

Table 2.9, *continued*

Option no.		GP ranking	Commission ranking	Implement- ation year
2.4	Brief interventions	33 =	49	–
8.6	Communication service	35	20	–
7.3	Assisted conception	36 =	38	–
6.5	Oral hygiene	36 =	44	–
3.3	Skin cancer prevention	36 =	32	–
6.3	Needle exchange	39 =	30	–
2.8	Detection and treatment of depression	39 =	48	2
6.4	Oral health education	41	39	–
1.7	Safety aids	42	27	–
3.4	Early recognition of skin cancer	43	34	–
4.3	Targeted stroke prevention	44	46	1
1.2	Immediate care	45 =	25	–
2.2	LBHU	45 =	47	4
8.5	Dietetics	47	42	–
1.5	Multiagency prevention	48	9	2
1.6	Prevention information	49	23	–

implemented in the first two years despite rankings above number 20 on the commission's list.

Approach to disinvestment

During the discussions, consideration was given to whether funds could be freed through disinvestments to increase the number of options implemented. A health economist (Dr James Raftery) proposed several alternatives:

1 Targeting specific ineffective or less effective treatments and ceasing to purchase them or purchasing less of them – so-called 'death lists' which, in a typical marginal analysis exercise, would be needed to balance out the 'wish lists' of investments.

2 Efficiency savings achieved by the purchaser imposing contract price reductions and creating incentives for providers to tackle the

technical inefficiencies in their provision of services. This could be either in the form of an 'across the board' percentage cut in prices or targeted more sensitively at areas where contract information showed potential for savings.

3 Redeployment within programmes as a result of shifting to new models of care, for example from acute to community rehabilitation. Several of the 49 options involved redeployments of this type.

During the discussion which followed, commission members seemed to share Dr Raftery's view that 'death lists' of procedures would not be likely to be a successful approach. While research data were improving as a result of various initiatives over recent years (such as the Effective Health Care Bulletins produced at York and widely disseminated through the NHS), there were very few treatments which were totally ineffective for all people, and the difficulty of gaining clinical and public support for disinvestment was considerable.

Some commission members felt that their job was to maximize the potential of the service to cure people and found discussion of disinvestment 'death lists' distasteful. Others disagreed, taking the view that wasting resources on less effective treatments was immoral.

It was also pointed out that evidence of effectiveness (or utility) was not the only factor to be considered: equity of access to health care and responsiveness to need were important too. For example, assisted conception techniques such as IVF might be relatively ineffective, but they often represented the only thing the health service could do to help needy couples, and a decision to deny treatment seemed very harsh. Similarly, grommets as a treatment for glue ear might be limited in their effectiveness, but for some they helped, and these might be the most needy sector of the population.

'Death lists' were not discarded out of hand, but were felt to be limited in their scope to yield substantial resources for redeployment. Dr Raftery preferred to advocate pursuit of greater efficiency in the provision of services (technical efficiency) as inefficiency was easier to demonstrate, harder to defend and, in his opinion, still rife.

This approach would require much better and more creative use of available information by purchasers. For example, Dr Raftery produced data which indicated that Southampton has a high hospitalization rate. The findings were based on the number of finished consultant episodes (FCEs), the term used for items of service performed by hospital doctors. With a rate of 155 FCEs per 1000 population, Southampton stands 10% above the national average and is the highest in its region. This may not of itself be inappropriate, but certainly suggested scope for analysis.

The commission concluded that more work should be done to clarify the scope for disinvestment along the lines proposed by Dr Raftery. A fuller discussion of this approach is presented in Chapter 4 of this book (see pages 90–106).

Without doubt, Southampton has hitherto felt less pressure to pursue disinvestment strategies because it has been relatively fortunate in the amount of growth money it has received each year, enabling most priorities for new investment to be funded without the need to adopt more radical approaches. In the post-1992 election years, this has been the case for many NHS purchasers (outside the London implementation zone) as noted by[8]. This situation may well be changing now, with the less generous settlement for the NHS in 1995–96 and the effects of the new funding formula[9], forcing purchasers such as Southampton to look closer at opportunities to disinvest.

Overview of procedure

This exercise in priority setting was much more complex than the simulation seminar performed earlier. In 1991, only 15 health investments were considered.

By contrast, this exercise involved 49 options. An attempt was made to consult not only the public but also other stakeholders. Cost data were prepared for each option.

Lessons learned from the earlier simulation seminar were partly responsible for the large number of options in this exercise. Because of the difficulties surrounding horizontal priority setting, it was felt that the best way to proceed was in the form of 'bite-sized chunks', and this was the method used in the years following the simulation seminar, developing detailed 'purchasing strategies' for particular health problems (stroke, mental health, etc.), which proposed new models of care and shifts of resources between acute and community care, for example. But for financial and other reasons, it had not been possible to implement all the programmes selected. That left a large number on the table. The new health commission did not want any prior short-listing done; it preferred to consider all the options itself.

The process was further complicated by the proactive approach taken to strategy. Instead of relying solely on bids from providers, the commission developed a health strategy of its own and this added to the number of options to be considered.

As a result, stakeholders as well as the commission itself found it difficult to set priorities. Only 72 replies were received from 375 stakeholders and 34 of these came from GPs. Nevertheless, the exercise impressed stakeholders with the difficult task facing the commission. Although they liked to be consulted, they seemed to prefer to leave the hard choices to the commission.

Deciding criteria

The main task facing the commission was to decide the criteria it wanted to use and it agreed on five: health gain, equity, choice, local access and personal responsibility. All these terms needed further definition and that applied particularly to the concepts of health gain and equity. Should they be considered from the standpoint of the individual or from the population at large?

Value for money (or cost-effectiveness) was agreed to be important but, as it turned out, too few relevant data were available to help with ranking the 49 options.

The main discussion centred on the priority to be assigned to health gain and equity. This was reflected both in the trial run that preceded the exercise as well as in the fishbowl discussion conducted by experts. The economists favoured a utilitarian approach, giving preference to options that produced the greatest good for the greatest number. The medical ethicist preferred an equity approach, giving everyone a right to all health care but allowing restrictions by clinicians dependent on an assessment of potential clinical benefit and funding considerations.

Disinvestment 'death lists' had been ruled out, but one of the economists suggested another way to secure more money for investing in priority options. That was to look at how the commission could apply leverage on providers so that they operate more efficiently. It remains to be seen whether this strategy will be successful.

The commission had tended to favour an equity approach in the past and that was the main message coming from stakeholders, particularly those who represented the public. But with securing population health benefit now the primary strategic purpose of commissions, health gain was given the greatest weight.

Ranking the options

The commission then tried two rankings: one based on the five weighted criteria, the other, incorporating the limited cost data available. Uncomfortable with these approaches, an entirely different method was tried.

The commission ranked options by health programme and then used the funding proportions it had set in the health strategy for each programme to produce its purchasing plan.

Furthermore, additional criteria had to be used that took account of such influences as past commitments and national targets. Implicit judgements greatly influenced the choices made throughout the whole process of priority setting, so much so that it was speculated that the same choices would have been made even if no discussion had been held. It would have been informative, in retrospect, to have asked commission members to rank the 49 options 'cold' before the exercise for comparison.

A five-year period was planned. Based on a high-growth funding assumption, 30 of the 49 options are scheduled to be implemented. However, in practice the growth assumptions may turn out to be overoptimistic and the programmes will almost certainly have to be trimmed. In this eventuality, the real value of the exercise will be realized as the agreed rankings provide a basis for trimming the programmes from the lowest priority upwards.

Ranking by health programme produced a radical change in the top 20 on the list. Choices were greatly influenced by past commitments and national targets. The commission had earlier tried to set priorities according to the 'pure' criteria of its mission statement, but, in the end, it had to take account of other considerations. This had the effect of making its final choices strikingly similar to those preferred by GPs.

References

1 Heginbotham C, Ham C, with Cochrane M, Richards J. (1992) *Purchasing Dilemmas – a Special Report from the King's Fund College and Southampton and South West Hampshire Health Authority.* King's Fund College, London.

2 Klein R, Redmayne S. (1992) *Patterns of Priorities: A Study of the Purchasing and Rationing Policies of Health Authorities.* NAHAT Research Paper No. 7. NAHAT, Birmingham.

3 Ham C. (1991) Revisiting the internal market and finding its all gone slow. *British Medical Journal* **301**: 250–1.

4 NHS Management Executive. (1990) *Developing Districts.* NHS, London.

5 Reports from the 'Rubber Windmill' simulations. *Contracting for Health Outcomes* (1990), *One Year On: Assuring Health Gain* (1991), *Planning to Achieve Health Gain* (1992). Cambridge: East Anglian Regional Health Authority/ Office for Public Management.

6 Welsh Health Planning Forum. (1989) *Strategic Intent and Direction for the NHS in Wales.* Welsh Office NHS Directorate, Cardiff.

7 Secretary of State for Health. (1991) *Health of the Nation.* HMSO, London.

8 Le Grand J. (1994) Evaluating the NHS reforms. In Robinson R, Le Grand J (eds). *Evaluating the NHS Reforms.* King's Fund Institute, London.

9 Smith P, Sheldon TA, Carr-Hill RA, Martin S, Peacock S, Hardman G. (1994) Allocating resources to health authorities: results and policy implications of small area analysis of use of in-patient services. *British Medical Journal* **309**: 1050–4.

3   Lessons learned

What lessons can be learned from the Southampton experience?
What did it reveal about priority setting that can be applied
elsewhere? How relevant is it?

Relevance of the Southampton experience

This exercise dealt with priority setting mainly as it applies to
growth money. Southampton is a gaining district and the commission
had the task of deciding how to allocate the funds available. Only a
limited effort was made to shift the balance of spending on existing
services. Funding proportions were set by programme, but the
pressure to pursue disinvestments was felt less severely than in
resource-losing districts.

Had the commission been forced to deal with cuts in funding,
different methods might have been employed. Some authorities faced
with cuts have seen fit to ring-fence funds for the chronic sick and to
concentrate the effects of the cuts on the acute sector. The
development of separate mental health and community service
trusts has reduced the need for such action, but cuts still present
special priority setting problems.

It seems likely that the methods employed in this exercise are
relevant to others. Gaining districts are faced with the pressing
need to make choices at the margin and they have a clearer field

in which to act. Resource-losing districts have more incentive to deal purposefully with disinvestment.

No quick fix

Priority setting has long been recognized as a difficult task, and the exercise demonstrated again that there is no quick fix. Processes are in a state of flux and health authorities will have to inch their way along an uncertain path.

It is doubtful if a 'right' solution or even a 'right' process will ever be realized. A large element of subjective judgement is involved no matter what process is used and some 'gut feeling' is unavoidable. But with relevant data and the help of experts, informed judgements can be developed.

The best to be expected is that health authorities make every effort to be just and fair. To do that, the process has to be exposed to public view, with well-defined procedures that reveal the values applied.

Coping with many options

Too many options were involved for the Southampton Commission as well as its stakeholders to consider comfortably. Both found it difficult to deal with more than five to ten options at a time. Similar findings arose from an exercise in Mid-Glamorgan[1]. For various reasons, 49 options were under consideration, but they were the result of selections made in eight health programmes, and ten options were the most involved in any programme. Priorities could be set more easily by programme, and in the end it was decided to do it that way. The funding proportions or 'formula shares' allocated for each programme were then used to produce an overall ranking. This method resembles the one devised in Oregon, where 17 categories of care had to be employed in order to cope with the huge number of condition–treatment pairs.

Other methods can be used to reduce the number of options considered for growth funding. The usual procedure is to solicit bids from providers and then have staff prepare a short list for health authorities to consider. Usually, only about ten to 20 options are selected. But this begs the question of what criteria are used to create the short-list.

Southampton preferred to follow a more proactive procedure and prepare a health strategy of its own. The commission also preferred to do the short-listing itself rather than leave the task to the managers. In this way, the whole process was more open and accountable. This alone makes the exercise a worthwhile one.

Though the commission was anxious to devote growth money to each programme, it wanted some to benefit more than others. Table 2.7 (see page 50) showed that it succeeded: 15 of the first 25 options to be implemented came from only three of the eight programmes.

Rational planning

Southampton did not rely on bids from providers. By developing a health strategy of its own, it pursued a proactive and rational planning policy which linked needs assessment more closely with purchasing decisions. Southampton thus set an example for other authorities to consider.

Many of the options produced by the exercise were the result of strategy work focusing on particular health problems, with consideration given mainly to their contribution to health gain. Other criteria may need more attention. This applies particularly to equity. Furthermore, commission members were not comfortable in applying purely utilitarian principles to their decisions. They felt a duty to safeguard the founding principles of equity enshrined in the NHS Act.

Bids were still presented by providers, but they were in the business plan form usually employed, showing only the cost and resources required. In future, providers will be asked to demonstrate how their bids contribute to health gain.

They will have to indicate how their proposals fit into the purchaser's framework and meet the criteria by which options are judged. However, rationality in planning can only go so far. When it comes to decision making on priorities, this exercise shows that the commission had to rely on informed judgement to a significant degree. It is the authors' opinion that this was not simply a result of having insufficient information of the right kind. Rather, it is the very nature of this kind of decision which cannot be purely rational, as other authors have frequently recognized[2].

Limited cost–utility data rule out marginal analysis

Cost–utility data are limited. In Southampton, QALY data were available for only ten of the 49 options. All that could be used were the estimated costs of implementation. No figures were available for two options, and only rough estimates could be given for others. Effectiveness data are also limited and often fail to take account of the quality of service[3]. Allowance must also be made for the place where treatment is to be given. Teaching hospitals or units that specialize in the treatment under consideration are more likely to produce the expected effects. The strength of the evidence behind options should be shown.

This means that marginal analysis techniques cannot be exclusively employed. Cost–utility data may be useful to deal with 'vertical' priorities but not 'horizontal' priorities.

Marginal analysis may be too narrowly focused if it deals only with efficiency. It needs to indicate who loses and who gains so that it can consider equity as well.

Needs assessment essential

Priorities are strongly influenced by an assessment of needs. Teenage pregnancy is a problem in Southampton, and this largely explains the high rankings (six and seven) given to two options – education and contraception clinics for teenagers and sex education in schools.

National targets exerted a strong influence because epidemiological studies showed profiles of the local population similar to those which apply to the country as a whole. Pressure also stemmed from Southampton's corporate contract with the region.

Marginal analysis has been suggested[4] as an alternative to whole needs assessment, but this did not apply in Southampton, and it probably does not elsewhere because of the difficulty in practice of identifying clearly just where the 'margin' is in health care (see page 34).

Clearer definition of criteria

The criteria used to set priorities need to be carefully defined. What is meant by 'health gain'? Does it apply to populations or individuals? Ideally, it should assess the quality as well as the length of life – adding life to years as well as years to life. But here, too, data are limited and rough judgements have to be made. A subjective element is involved in the assessment of the effectiveness of treatment as well as its cost.

Health gain is a nebulous concept when applied to the chronic sector. How do you measure the relief of suffering or an integrated approach to teenage pregnancy? Process rather than outcome measures have to be used.

Equity also needs to be defined. Does it relate to the rights of individuals or groups? If the latter, is it concerned with access to local services (a concern particularly of rural populations) or the availability of services to ethnic minorities and deprived groups?

What is meant by criteria such as choice and personal responsibility? Does choice mean a choice of services or a choice of location? Does personal responsibility deal with who caused the illness or who should pay for it?

Assigning weights to criteria

In the mid-Glamorgan exercise, no way could be found to rank the importance of criteria. Southampton did it by assigning weights for each of the five main criteria under consideration. The weights were based on judgements made by commission members. To allow greater scope for scoring, they were asked to allot 100 points across the five criteria. An average was then taken of the weights assigned.

However, no attempt was made to repeat the exercise when other criteria were added. Such matters as national targets and past commitments applied only to particular options and thus did not lend themselves to point scoring. They were considered only where relevant.

The commission demonstrated a strong commitment to its mission and aims, but found that closer examination showed the need to balance these ideals with pragmatic considerations, especially the 'givens' of national policy.

Health gain versus equity

Health gain and equity are emerging as the two main criteria employed. The former is favoured by utilitarian health economists who stress the need for health authorities to live within budgets and provide the greatest good for the greatest number. Their approach is utilitarian.

Equity is favoured by philosophers and ethicists who are concerned with individual rights. They see health in social terms and define disability widely, taking account of mental as well as physical effects.

One way of reconciling the concepts of health gain and equity may be by allowing greater funding for extracontractual referrals. This would permit individual rights to be considered when local services are not available, but it appears merely to duck the difficult choices facing purchasers.

No clear way to relate criteria to choices

Ultimately, no clear way was found to relate criteria to choices; 'gut feelings' may have exerted considerable influence.

An attempt to relate criteria to options was made with only one health programme, but it produced conflicting results. When these same choices were included in the ranking of all 49 options, a different order resulted. Similarly, ranking of all 49 criteria by five weighted criteria conflicted with those produced by one which considered available costs.

Equally uncertain is the influence exerted by experts. Their fishbowl discussion sharpened differences between criteria but may not have affected the way options were ranked. Normally, of course, a commission would not make use of expert opinion in this way – in any case, during the preparation of purchasing plan. More thought should be given to the kind of advice, especially ethical advice, which such decision-makers need.

One way to assess criteria influence is by a before and after method. Commission members were not asked to rank options before the discussion began. If this had been done, then the order could have been compared with the ranks finally assigned. It might then have been possible to see if the discussion had any influence on the selection and weighting of criteria.

Pragmatic criteria strongly influence rankings

Rankings may be influenced by other criteria, particularly national targets and past commitments. Southampton could not ignore government targets, media exposure or the need to sustain previous developments. The extent to which options can be implemented in the time period involved also has to be considered.

Complications also arise when other agencies, such as social services, are involved. If infrastructure costs are incurred, who is to bear them? When Southampton compared rankings based on the five weighted criteria and costs, it found differences between the rankings greatest when other funding agencies (such as social services) were involved.

Protection for chronic sick and deprived groups

Political and public pressures tend to focus on the acutely ill, making it difficult to give priority to the chronic sick and deprived groups such as the mentally ill. It is also hard to assess outcome and effectiveness of treatment in this sector, thereby obscuring credit for health gain.

Southampton had top priorities for stroke, mental health and community care for the elderly, but national targets and public preference forced high rankings for options designed to reduce waiting lists and improve emergency services. Community teams for the mentally ill had the highest ranking but the large amount of money involved meant that the option could be implemented only if other programmes received comparatively less growth funding.

Some form of ring-fenced financing may be needed to ensure sufficient funding for vulnerable groups and prevent diversion to the acute sector.

As a result of the NHS and Community Care Act, responsibility for the chronic sick and vulnerable groups has been largely shifted to social services. If bed stays are cut, this increases the load on carers. Some means of ascertaining social service views are needed before health authorities make choices

Stakeholder consultation necessary and needs more care

The lack of sufficient time and space to explore stakeholder views was a weakness of the process. Holding a consultation over the summer meant that many respondents were put under unreasonable pressure to give a considered response. The commission also probably needed more time to understand the key messages from the survey. Although the actual number of responses was low (72 of 375 questionnaires), it must be emphasized that coverage of different stakeholder groups was fair and that many stakeholders made a *corporate* response (e.g. provider trusts, councils for community services) meaning that numbers of respondents was less important than what they said.

The public's role

It seems that the public likes to be consulted but it wants health authorities to make the hard choices. It can help to produce the values or criteria that underpin priorities but it does not have the information or expertise needed to make specific choices.

Values or criteria can best be elicited by means of case vignettes presented to focus groups. General public meetings are poorly attended and difficult to organize. In developing options for health authorities to consider, user groups can provide useful information. This is probably the most valuable form that public consultation can take.

Some form of public consultation is needed to test assent to health authority priorities. If the process is exposed to public view, the difficulties of priority setting can be displayed and the public is more likely to have confidence in the fairness of the decisions taken. That can be ascertained by providing a consultation procedure at the end of the process as well as at the beginning. That would give the public a chance to express its reaction to the priorities finally chosen.

The public may understand if health authorities focus on health gain but its interest tends to centre on other considerations. In many ways, this is a natural suggestion, as the public expects the health service to provide effective treatments to whoever needs them and to maintain standards of clinical quality. Equity in the distribution of resources among people is also largely assumed − certainly the 'old' NHS is held by most to have embodied this principle. What concerns there are may arise from fears about consequences of the reforms and 'market-type' incentives for providers and GPs. This assumption of equity may be misplaced and requires testing. Chapter 4 (*see* pages 80−9 and 114−120) develops this theme further.

Major considerations for public consultees and many other stakeholders are the questions of *choice* and *access* (especially with regard to waiting, but also the 'localness' of services), judging by the high scores attributed in the stakeholder consultation to options which were strong on these attributes. This follows from the postulation above: if it is *assumed* that effective services will be available to all in response to their needs, it only remains to have concern over one's right to exercise choice and not to be kept waiting.

The public finds it easier to suggest service developments than to propose or accept cuts. However, restriction rather than cessation of services may be more acceptable. This was evident in the mid-Glamorgan exercise. The public was reluctant to consider disinvestments but it did accept the need for fewer services in some areas such as ultrasound for pregnant women.

GPs can help decide priorities

GPs have the information and expertise needed to set priorities. Many of their choices coincided with those of the Southampton Commission. While the public may help to develop the criteria used to underpin priorities, GPs have the expertise and experience needed to rank options. Because of their gatekeeper role and referral decisions, they exert considerable influence on the way resources are used. Indeed, if the strategies of commissions are to continue to have relevance, they must reflect more carefully the priorities of GPs in future.

More involvement by provider groups

Providers and professional advisory bodies were consulted during the development of the health strategy, and some participated in the stakeholder consultation. A neurosurgeon and a psychogeriatrician were included among the experts in the fishbowl exercise, thereby giving the acute and chronic sectors of care a chance to express their views.

But no other providers were present at commission proceedings when priorities were being considered. In the mid-Glamorgan exercise, criteria were set by core group teams which included public and provider representatives as well as purchasers.

Questions were raised during commission proceedings which only providers could answer. However, their presence can inhibit discussion and distort priorities. Some alternative means of consultation may be needed.

Efficiency before exclusions

Before services are excluded, an attempt should be made to secure more efficient operation. Southampton learned that by more creative use of the abundant information produced by the contracting process, there may yet be considerable scope for greater technical efficiency from providers. More work is proceeding in this area.

Before the process began in New Zealand, an inventory was taken of 20 common conditions to find out where money was being spent. This made it possible to concentrate efficiency efforts on those areas where they would produce the greatest saving.

Disinvestments cannot always be ignored

Exclusions were ruled out because of data deficiencies and fear of media reaction. A concern for equity was also a factor. If cutbacks were needed, the commission preferred to do it, curtailing unnecessary referrals or restricting access rather than terminating services completely.

With growth money at its disposal, Southampton did not feel under great pressure to identify disinvestments. Some districts are not so fortunately placed and hard choices have had to be made if new priorities are to be met. Southampton itself may find this necessary in future years.

References

1 Cohen D. (1994) Marginal analysis in practice: an alternative to needs assessment for contracting health care. *British Medical Journal* **309:** 781–5.
2 Moore PG. (1993) *The Business of Risk*. Cambridge University Press, Cambridge.
3 Hurley S. (1992) Indices of therapeutic outcome in pharmaco-economic evaluation of drug therapy. *Pharmaco-economics* **1:** 155–60.
4 Mooney G, Gerard K, Donaldson C, Farrar S. (1992) *Priority Setting In Purchasing: Some Practical Guidelines*. National Association of Health Authorities and Trusts, Birmingham.

4　Emergent themes

In this part of the book, various authors offer their personal observations on some wider themes which emerge from, or are illustrated by, the Purchasing Dilemmas exercise. These include contributions from the panel of experts who took part in the event, the chairman and non-executives of the commission, and managers working in the commission on these issues.

Some of the papers are reflective, others speculative. The views expressed do not necessarily represent those of any organization, but are personal to the authors.

Ray Robinson and Len Doyal, in turn, present the alternative frameworks offered by a 'Benthamite' utilitarian approach (maximum benefit to the greatest number of people) and an egalitarian approach based on human rights. The interplay between these arguments is at the heart of the difficulties faced in priority setting.

Tony Lockett, James Raftery and John Richards examine the methods of programme budgeting and marginal analysis, questioning particularly their applicability to disinvestment, and suggesting how this work will be taken forward in Southampton.

Colin Godber, Lawrence Maule and Jo Ash comment on the usefulness and validity of the approach adopted in Southampton from their different viewpoints. They examine the role of the commission and their expectations of it.

John Richards and Tony Lockett cast an eye to the future, especially in the light of the government's 'primary care led purchasing' initiative, and speculate on the nature of the strategic role commissions may need to adopt.

Peter Lees and Nick Allen reflect on the nature of the purchaser–provider relationship created by the NHS reforms, and suggest the need for a more mature relationship based on collaboration if the community is to see real benefits.

Finally, the non-executive members of the commission reflect on their role in decision making, the benefits of the Purchasing Dilemmas exercise and the added value they seek to bring to commissioning.

Health economics and priority setting: nonsense on stilts?

Ray Robinson

'Nonsense on stilts' was a phrase used 20 years ago by Professor Peter Self to describe his view of the contribution made by economists to the cost–benefit study of the then proposed third London airport[1]. A similar view is taken by some commentators about the role of health economics in relation to the task of NHS priority setting. Not surprisingly, as an economist, I do not share this view. Hard decisions have to be taken about the allocation of scarce resources and the economists' approach – which endeavours to identify and measure the full range of costs and consequences associated with available options – represents a valuable aid to decision making.

Of course there have been a number of well-documented debates about the ethical basis of the economists' utilitarian approach, especially when it involves the use of outcome measures such as quality adjusted life years (QALYs)[2,3]. QALYs have also been accused of discriminating against elderly people, making illegitimate inter-personal comparisons, disregarding equity considerations and introducing bias into quality of life scales[4-8]. However, this ground is well covered and so I do not propose to dwell on it here. Instead I want to address a rather more insidious threat, one that could lead to disenchantment with the economists' approach among practitioners if it is not addressed.

What is the danger?

Nowadays it seems almost obligatory that policy documents coming from the Department of Health should contain some reference to the need for cost-effectiveness to be taken into account when making decisions about resource allocation. Moreover, the message has percolated down the system to the extent that individual health authority documents, such as health strategies and purchasing plans, are littered with references to the 'cost-effectiveness' of the authority's preferred options. On one level this is entirely desirable. Economic evaluation is concerned with making the best use of scarce health care resources and cost-effectiveness analysis is one form of economic evaluation. Surely a methodology which takes account of the full range of cost and consequences of all the options under review can but improve decision making? My own view is yes, in theory, but not always in practice. It is the mismatch between expectations based upon theory and the reality of practice which threatens to discredit economic evaluation.

The case of QALYs

To illustrate this point consider the contribution to health care decision making offered through the use of cost–utility analysis, especially the use of QALYs. QALYs are a particularly powerful measure of health outcome because they combine quantitative features (i.e. the number of life years gained from a particular intervention) with qualitative aspects (i.e. the quality of life in each year) in order to obtain a composite index of outcome. Comparisons between alternative interventions or programmes can then be based on the marginal cost per QALY gained from each of them.

Numerous QALY-based studies have been carried out involving particular procedures and programmes[9] and a guide on how to use the approach has been produced[10]. Drawing on this type of work, Maynard[11] recently published a league table which purported to show the relative value for money, in terms of cost per QALY, obtained from alternative health care interventions (Table 4.1).

The ultimate use of such a QALY league table is to offer guidance in relation to resource allocation decisions, that is to show how resources could be shifted away from those areas where the cost per QALY is high towards those areas where it is low and a better rate of

Table 4.1 Maynard's QALY league table

Treatment	Cost per QALY (£ August, 1990)
Cholesterol testing and diet therapy only (all adults aged 40–69)	220
Neurosurgical intervention for head injury	240
Advice to stop smoking from general practitioner	270
Neurosurgical intervention for subarachnoid haemorrhage	490
Antihypertensive treatment to prevent stroke (ages 45–64)	940
Pacemaker implantation	1100
Hip replacement	1180
Valve replacement for aortic stenosis	1140
Cholesterol testing and treatment	1480
Coronary artery bypass graft (left main vessel disease, severe angina)	2090
Kidney transplant	4710
Breast cancer screening	5780
Heart transplantation	7840
Cholesterol testing and treatment (incrementally) of all adults aged 25–39	14150
Home haemodialysis	17260
Coronary artery bypass graft (one-vessel disease, moderate angina)	18830
Continuous ambulatory peritoneal dialysis	19870
Hospital haemodialysis	21970
Erythropoietin treatment for anaemia in dialysis patients (assuming 10% reduction in mortality)	54380
Neurosurgical intervention for malignant intracranial tumours	107780
Erythropoietin treatment for anaemia in dialysis patients (assuming no increase in survival)	126290

Source: Maynard[11].

return is obtainable. However, following the appearance of this table, a number of health economists issued warnings about the hazards of interpreting such tables. Reservations were expressed about the often poor-quality data and inadequate methods that had been used in some studies; about the difficulties of comparing studies undertaken in different years when different technologies and prices prevailed; about the use of different measures of health outcomes; and about the inappropriateness of transferring results obtained in one local setting to another[12,13]. Elsewhere, Maynard himself has raised questions about reliability of the measures of clinical effectiveness upon which many cost per QALY studies have been based[14]. The combined effect of these criticisms has been to throw considerable doubt upon the reliability of extant knowledge in relation to cost per QALY evidence.

An alternative approach

In response to these criticisms, some health economists have recommended a modified form of economic evaluation as a practical aid to decision making. This approach involves a combination of programme budgeting and marginal analysis (PBMA)[15,16]. The fundamental aim of PBMA is to provide a framework for decision making without seeking the precision, and data requirements, of the cost per QALY approach. It uses the general cost–benefit framework as a means of organizing the information that is available and clarifying what alternative choices will entail. That is, it makes explicit the trade-offs which exist between different packages of care (see Box 1). The Southampton purchasing dilemmas project employed a modified form of PBMA.

Box 1 Steps in PBMA

- Define programmes
- Estimate programme budgets
- Define subprogrammes
- Identify margins
- Draw up incremental and decremental wish lists
- Identify marginal costs/benefits associated with wish list activities
- Set priorities

Source: Mooney et al.[15]

Even in this modified form, however, the application of the cost–

benefit framework poses a number of problems. Three of these are mentioned here. First, there is the problem of the information overload facing decision-makers. In the Southampton case, the health commission members were faced with 49 options for investment over the next five years. Even with the organizing framework offered by PBMA, members' ability to absorb the range of information associated with such a large and diverse set of options was clearly limited. Second, a problem remained in relation to data availability. Despite restricting the data requirements to broad measures of effectiveness and cost-effectiveness, the necessary QALY-type data were only available for ten of the 49 options. Third, the exercise confirmed most vividly how health commissions need to balance multiple objectives, and how pragmatic and political considerations come into play. In this connection, a related point arose in relation to the difficulty of achieving consensus about disinvestment strategy. Vested interests and political considerations played a large part here. Recognition of this fact has led some economists to recommend concentration on maximizing the technical efficiency of providers rather than seeking to achieve allocative efficiency in the case of disinvestment strategies.

The way forward

What lessons can be learned from the general experience of applying methods of economic evaluation in health authority priority setting and the specific experience of Southampton and South West Hampshire Health Commission? The difficulties cited above may be taken by some people to imply that the economist's approach contains some fatal flaws. In my opinion, however, such a view would be mistaken. A more balanced judgement is required.

To start with, it should be emphasized that major progress has been made over the last ten years in the development of methods of economic evaluation in health care. Among health economists a consensus is emerging about the methodologies to be employed, although a number of unresolved areas still remain[17]. Despite all this progress, however, the number of studies that have been carried out remains strictly limited. Hutton[18] has referred to economic evaluation as a 'half-way technology'. As such, it is important to continue to develop research and development in relation to economic evaluation, but to be open about the limitations of extant knowledge and, in the short term, not to place unrealistic expectations on the approach.

As far as PBMA is concerned, despite its limitations, it continues to offer a framework for improved decision making. It is explicit and makes policy trade-offs clear. This argument will have little appeal to those who believe in 'muddling through elegantly'[19]. But it should prove attractive to those who would like to see a larger element of rational, evidence-based decision making in health care.

Finally, the message for those who continue to emphasize the limitations of economic evaluation is that the onus is upon them to produce something demonstrably superior. In the words of the Economics Nobel Laureate, Milton Friedman: 'You need a candidate to beat a candidate'.

References

1 Self P. (1975) *Ecnocrats and the policy process.* Macmillan, London.

2 Hadorn DC. (1991) Setting health priorities in Oregon. *Journal of American Medical Association,* **265**: 2218–26.

3 Williams A. (1994) *Economics, QALYs and Medical Ethics. A Health Economist's Perspective.* Discussion Paper 121. Centre for Health Economics, University of York.

4 Broome J. (1987) Good, fairness and QALYs. In Bell M, Medus S (eds). *Proceedings of the Royal Institute of Philosophy Conference on Philosophy and Medical Welfare.* Cambridge University Press, Cambridge.

5 Carr-Hill R. (1989) Assumptions of the QALY procedure. *Social Science and Medicine,* **29**: 469–77.

6 Carr-Hill R. (1991) Allocating resources to health care: is the QALY a technical solution to a political problem? *International Journal of Health Services,* **21**: 351–63.

7 Loomes G, McKenzie L. (1989) The use of QALYs in health care decision making. *Social Science and Medicine,* **28:** 299–308.

8 Wagstaff A. (1991) QALYs and the equity–efficiency trade-off. *Journal of Health Economics,* **10:** 21–41.

 9 Gerard K. (1991) *A Review of Cost–Utility Studies: Assessing their Policy Making Relevance.* Discussion Paper 11/91. Health Economics Research Unit and Departments of Public Health and Economics, University of Aberdeen, Aberdeen.
10 Gudex C, Kind P. (1988) The QALY toolkit, Discussion Paper 38. Centre for Health Economics, University of York.
11 Maynard A. (1991) Developing the health care market. *Economic Journal,* **101**: 1277–86.
12 Mason J, Drummond M, Torance G. (1993) Some guidelines on the use of cost-effectiveness league tables. *British Medical Journal,* **306**: 570–2.
13 Gerard K, Mooney G. (1993) QALY league tables: handle with care. *Health Economics,* **2**: 59–64.
14 Freemantle N, Maynard A. (1994) Something rotten in the state of clinical and economic evaluations? *Health Economics,* **3**: 63–67.
15 Mooney G, Gerard K, Donaldson C, Farrar S. (1992) *Priority Setting In Purchasing: Some Practical Guidelines.* National Association of Health Authorities and Trusts, Birmingham.
16 Cohen D. (1994) Marginal analysis in practice: an alternative to needs assessment for contracting health care. *British Medical Journal,* **309**: 781–5.
17 Rutten F, Drummond M. (1994) *Making Decisions about Health Technologies: A Cost-Effectiveness Perspective.* Centre for Health Economics, University of York.
18 Hutton J. (1994) Economic evaluation of health care: a halfway technology. *Health Economics* **3**: 1–4.
19 Hunter D. (1993) *Rationing Dilemmas in Health Care.* NAHAT, Birmingham.

How not to ration health care: the moral perils of utilitarian decision making

Len Doyal

In their new role as purchasers, health authorities are addressing the question of how scarce health care resources should be rationed. The National Health Service was created to provide equal access to medical treatment on the basis of equal need. How should this principle of equality be interpreted in the face of shortages in health care resources? In debates about this issue, two conflicting approaches have received support.

According to the first – a form of utilitarianism – the principle of equality should be given up. When resources are scarce, it makes more sense to allocate them in ways which will benefit the largest number of people, recognizing that there is not enough to go around for everyone. Such judgements might be made on the grounds of cost-effectiveness or public preference or both. The second approach rejects this view and regards appropriate health care as an individual right which cannot be trumped by the interests of the majority, however these may be defined. So long as a satisfiable individual need for health care resources exists then it should either be satisfied or stand an equal chance of being satisfied.

In this paper, utilitarian approaches to health care rationing will be criticized and a rights-based approach defended. This defence will argue that to deny that rationing must occur on a playing field of equal access to health care is irrational and conflicts with some of our most cherished moral beliefs. The practical implications of this argument will be explored through the development of a general model of equitable purchasing, one which does not have to resort to utilitarian injustice or to collapse into utopianism through turning its back on the inevitability of rationing health care.

Human need and the right to appropriate health care

The concept of human need is central to the moral foundation of the NHS. To evolve as humans – to flourish in the sense of having the opportunity to achieve those things we wish to attempt and of which we are capable – we must be able to participate in social activity with others. Such participation requires the satisfaction of certain basic needs. One of these is physical health. To the degree that this is absent then our capacity for social interaction will be impaired. As a result, we will be disabled – unable to do our best at whatever we and others believe it important for us to try to achieve[1].

This view of basic human need helps us to understand why humans have a universal right to good health care. The existence of a basic need such as physical health does not in itself create the right to its satisfaction. The link between basic needs and rights is created by our belief that the person in need has moral duties[2]. Generally speaking, this is what we all believe of each other – that being a citizen of our society goes hand in hand with accepting moral order. The removal of individuals from society or their punishment in some other way is often seen to be justified if they fail to do what is perceived to be their duty.

Yet we cannot have it both ways. The corollary of this argument is that if we want individuals to do what we believe to be right then they are entitled to the goods and services which enable them to do their best to make and act on the appropriate choices. Otherwise, they will not feel that they have the same moral stake in society that we do. Suppose that someone has an acute or chronic illness for which treatment is available but which she is not receiving and cannot provide for herself. She will directly experience the contradiction of losing her physical or mental independence and self-sufficiency in a social environment which places moral priority on both. If the other members of her community do nothing to provide the care she needs, then why should she (or her relatives and friends) take them and their moral beliefs seriously[3]?

Persons ignored in this way might feel morally and socially disenfranchised, and for good reason. Indeed, the increases in crime and violence in the most deprived areas of our society are directly related to such sentiments. Things will not improve unless the equal right of all citizens to basic need satisfaction – in this case to appropriate health care – is respected. This is because, when we discriminate in the provision of health care (or education or housing), we are proclaiming that we value the lives of some more than others. Moreover, when we condone such inequalities, we create the conditions for potential discrimination against ourselves. We too may become ill and fall on hard times. In short, if we expect others to do what we believe to be morally right, including valuing *our* own lives and capabilities, then we should respect the equal right of everyone to appropriate health care.

Although the reasons for its evolution are complex, the National Health Service can be seen as the institutional embodiment of this line of moral reasoning[4]. Its guiding principle of equal access based on equal need is one driven not by income or charity but by right. Access to appropriate health care should not depend on the precariousness and arbitrariness of wealth or popularity with others. The degree to which the importance of this right is accepted throughout Britain is confirmed by the general popularity of the NHS across political boundaries.

Yet the fact remains that health care resources are scarce – not everyone can have everything they need at the moment they need it, much less everything they want. The NHS is underfunded and one of the most urgent problems facing purchasing authorities is how to manage the scarcity which this creates. How then should we decide who gets what and when?

Justifying inequality: utilitarian approaches to rationing

As we have seen, utilitarian approaches to prioritizing spending on health care depart from the traditional emphasis within the NHS on equal access based on equal need. Utilitarians argue that because of scarcity everyone cannot have an equal right to health care. Rights cannot exist unless there is an individual or institution on which their claim can be realistically made. Since at present there are not enough resources to go around, a minority of people who are less deserving will just have to wait longer for treatment than others, possibly having to forgo it altogether. Otherwise, it is argued, it will be impossible to optimize the benefits of available treatments – the health gains – for the majority of individuals who are agreed to deserve them most.

Two different utilitarian approaches to rationing have been advocated[5]. The first focuses on the volume of health gain to be achieved, arguing that health care resources should be allocated in proportion to anticipated benefits weighed against costs. A Quality Adjusted Life Year (QALY) is the tool most commonly associated with the measure of such cost-effectiveness. Here health gain is defined with reference to increases in life expectancy and physical mobility and decreases in pain. Treatments are then prioritized on the basis of those which are perceived to provide the most benefit for the least money. It follows that, when resources are depleted, some people who require the treatment deemed to be least cost effective should receive nothing. Such inequalities are then morally tolerated rather than denying health care to those who can derive most benefit from it[6].

The second utilitarian approach to rationing also accepts that the collective benefit of the majority can trump the rights of the individual. But here the argument is that the general public should decide how spending priorities should be established. This is to be done through a system of extensive consultation where the resulting decisions might or might not be cost effective in the preceding terms. Here, the central idea is that it is morally right that 'the people' should collectively choose how their taxes should be spent on health care. They or their representatives might do this either through prioritizing treatments deemed most worthy or through agreeing the criteria by which such priorities should be decided[7]. An example of the former is the policy behind the current provision of Medicaid in Oregon[8]. The latter is illustrated by the process undertaken last year in Southampton, on which this volume is based.

According to either of these utilitarian arguments, the rationing of health care should therefore be based on the maximization of benefit linked to cost-effectiveness or on the preferences of the majority. Ideally, it should be based on both. Such arguments might appear to provide a moral justification for discriminating against the minority in the service of the majority. However, their moral price is very high indeed.

As regards the estimation of cost–benefit, tools such as QALYs do not only face well-known methodological problems[9]. If they are used to justify rationing, we confuse the empirical fact of such an estimate with the moral appropriateness of employing it to determine the value of the life and health of any individual. It does not follow from the fact that you may have an illness which is difficult and expensive to treat that your disabilities should be treated as any less significant than those faced by individuals who can more cheaply and efficiently be provided with medical care.

If health authorities adopt such policies, they proclaim that, through no fault of their own, some individuals are worth less than others. Such a principle of inequality challenges the moral fabric of our society – the belief in the equality of humans and the respect which they are due because they are humans, irrespective of their individual characteristics[10].

Things do not improve when we move to the second utilitarian justification for discriminatory rationing. To deny an individual appropriate health care because a majority has judged it morally acceptable to do so is to learn nothing from the outrages of history. The fact that a majority of people have made a decision does not ensure its moral rightness. Indeed, there are numerous examples of situations where majorities have knowingly supported policies towards minorities which were clearly immoral. Moreover, majorities can be misled by poor information and by poorly organized decision-making processes. Decisions which are supposedly representative of democratic wishes may not in fact be so. They can also be distorted by secrecy, corruption and the influence of vested interests. Thus democratic decisions can be both immoral and irrational.

The purchasing priorities which some health authorities have drawn up after supposed consultation with the general public illustrate these problems. Infertility, for example, can be a shattering experience for those who experience it. To be unable to have biological children can be a profoundly depressing and debilitating experience, especially for some women. Yet the public almost always rank IVF unfavourably in comparison with other treatments[11]. Interestingly, psychiatric treatment for serious mental illness also receives low ratings[12].

The fact of the unpopularity of such treatments provides no coherent moral justification for unequal constraints on their provision. To take another example of unpopular provision, suppose that a man is disabled by the facial tattoos which he inflicted upon himself when young and inebriated and is financially unable to get them removed. As a result, he is socially disabled – unable to get work and responsibly to care for himself and his family, something he desperately wishes to do.

Assume that the majority in his locality have declared tattoo removal unavailable on the NHS, denying him the cosmetic surgery he needs to do his best to conform to its shared morality[13]. Why should he wish to continue to be a responsible citizen in a society unwilling to provide him with the necessary conditions for doing so? A strong majority can force its utilitarian will upon a sick and disabled minority but only by undermining its own collective morality through not applying it to everyone in the same way.

A just allocation of resources

The common utilitarian response to criticisms of the above sort is that such moral high ground is all fine and good. However, all purchasers of health care must establish priorities – they cannot buy everything that might do some immediate good for everyone. There are just not enough resources to go around, especially when budgetary planning has to anticipate the need for future as well as current treatments and preventive strategies. If utilitarian criteria are rejected on the grounds that they violate the equal right to appropriate health care, their critics must provide alternative and reasonable policies for rationing which are not subject to the same charge[14]. The following is an outline of such a policy.

The rationing of health care will inevitably be discriminatory. This means that everyone will not be treated with the same degree of immediacy. The issue is whether or not we can find a way of organizing such discrimination so that its effects are equally and acceptably shared by all. We have already seen that it would be unjust to discriminate on the basis of *types* of treatment, whether in relation to their expense or their unpopularity. So long as illness entails genuine disability to participate in social life then it merits effective treatment – provided that this is technically feasible. A morally just health service must therefore maintain treatment for all categories of disabling illness. Human need rather than expense or popularity should dictate the purchase and provision of health care resources[15].

It follows that needs assessment should drive decisions about the general allocation of health care provision. Health authorities should go about this process in three ways:

1 For the designated population, an epidemiological evaluation of the proportional need for health care should be carried out. The tools of such evaluation are still crude and rely on a host of different types of information – everything from general data on mortality and morbidity, to previous levels of expenditure, to special studies focusing on the prevalence and seriousness of specific illnesses. On the basis of an aggregation of the results of such studies it should be possible to divide overall levels of need into rough percentage claims for health care resources, for example so much for heart disease as opposed to mental illness[16].

2 Careful analysis must be made of the effectiveness of existing interventions in health care, the potential satisfiers to be purchased for those needs shown to exist. However, the purpose

of such studies should not be to ration treatments on a scale of effectiveness. A treatment option which may not be particularly effective may still be the only one which marginally reduces the disability of a particular illness. Of course, treatments with no known efficacy should not be funded[17].

3 A top slice of the overall budget must occur for extracontractual referrals (ECRs), health promotion and research and development. While too complex an issue to consider here, the level of this top slicing should generally reflect strict appraisals of potential need as regards ECR provision and the potential success of other strategic initiatives concerning, among other things, health promotion and clinical and non-clinical research.

But surely, the utilitarian critic might respond, such a picture only makes the problem of rationing even more acute. If no existing component of health care provision is to be excised then each remaining component will have fewer resources than would otherwise be the case. This is true and brings us to our last strategy for rationing in conformity with the equal right of everyone to appropriate health care. If we should not ration *between* types of needed care, we have no choice but to ration *within* them. Can this be fairly done?

The answer is yes, provided that health authorities insist that their purchasing specifications conform to the following principles for everyone:

- There should be a form of triage based on immediacy and degree of need. This divides all patients into three categories of moral similarity and priority: acute, urgent or elective. Treatment should then be provided in this order – in the same way for everyone. This approach to rationing preserves the principle of equal access to services on the basis of degree of need and is already standard practice among health care providers[18].

- Patients within each of these categories of moral priority should be placed on waiting lists. Properly administered waiting lists preserve equality of access to treatment through providing individuals of morally similar levels of need with an equal chance of satisfaction. Who is treated first should be decided randomly on the basis of when they contracted their illness and how severe it happens to be.

- The fair construction and management of waiting lists should be a condition of the award of contracts for secondary care, along with clear policies as to how this is to be achieved and audited. Such audits would be designed, for example, to penalize the maintenance of long waits for conditions which are professionally unpopular to treat (e.g. varicose veins) but for which there is a cheap and effective remedy.

- Primary carers, whether or not they are fundholders, should also be accountable for the equity of their distribution of resources. Where available and when appropriate, their practices should be seen to conform to clinical guidelines for effective treatment and their patterns of referral should not be prejudicial to particular groups because of the expense or unpopularity of their illnesses.

- Decisions not to provide acute or life-saving treatment within an area of provision should always be made on clinical and not resource grounds. Clinical guidelines for this purpose should be agreed contractually with providers.

- Complaints procedures should also be improved to ensure that apparent injustices are heard and, if appropriate, corrected.

At present, this model of equitable purchasing is very generalized and too abstract. To be useful, much more elaboration is required to explore its practical implications for departments of public health, for the negotiation of block and more specific contracts with providers, for the allocation of ECRs and for the acceptability and management of waiting lists. Yet it is equally clear that there is nothing impractical about the model in principle. Were contracting, and the rationing that it inevitably entails, to be organized along these lines, it would not only be fair but would be seen to be fair by the general public. It might entail consequences which many would reject, for example the provision of treatment for IVF in proportion to need. However, the moral principles and arguments on which this and other decisions were based would be seen equally to apply to everyone.

Conclusion

When it is necessary, the rationing of health care should be based on the original moral foundation of the NHS: equal access on the basis of need. Utilitarian attempts to water down this principle through funding provision which is less expensive or more popular with the public are in breach of this principle. Their rejection does not entail a utopia in which rationing does not occur or where issues such as cost-effectiveness are dismissed. Equal and fair rationing can take place while keeping efficiency to the fore, and a model has been outlined for how this might be done. It would locate the discretion which purchasing inevitably entails within secure moral boundaries rather than leaving them to the mercy of poorly organized and unreflective 'democratic' debate.

References

1 Doyal L, Gough I. (1991) *A Theory of Human Need*, pp. 49–75. Macmillan, London.
2 Doyal L, Gough I. Ibid, pp. 91–115.
3 Bellamy, R. (1992) Liberal rights, socialist goals and the duties of citizenship. In Milligan D, Miller W (eds). *Liberalism, Citizenship and Autonomy*, pp. 88–107. Avebury, Aldershot.
4 Stacey M. (1988) *The Sociology of Health and Healing*, pp. 116–32. Unwin Hyman, London.
5 Bottomley V. (1993) Priority setting in the NHS. In *BMJ* (eds) *Rationing in Action*, pp. 25–32. BMJ, London.
6 Williams A. (1988) Ethics and efficiency in the provision of health care. In Bell J, Mendus S (eds). *Philosophy and Medical Welfare*, pp. 111–26. Cambridge University Press, Cambridge.
7 NHS Management Executive. (1992) *Local Voices*. HMSO, London.
8 Brannigan M. (1993) Oregon's experiment. *Health Care Analysis*, **1**: 15–32.
9 Mooney G. (1994) *Key Issues in Health Economics*, pp. 49–63. Harvester, London.
10 Harris, J. (1988) More and better justice. In Bell J, Mendus S (eds). *Philosophy and Medical Welfare*, pp. 75–90. Cambridge University Press, Cambridge.

11 Redmayne S, Klein R. (1993) Rationing in practice: the case of in vitro fertilisation. *British Medical Journal*, **306**: 1457–8.

12 Heginbotham, C. (1993) Health care priority setting: a survey of doctors, managers, and the general public. In *BMJ* (eds) *Rationing in Action*, pp. 141–56. BMJ, London.

13 Klein R, Redmayne S. (1992) *Patterns of Priorities*. NAHAT, Birmingham.

14 Maynard A. (1994) Prioritising health care – dreams and reality. In Malek M (ed.). *Setting Priorities in Health Care*, pp. 1–17. Wiley, London.

15 Doyal L. (1993) The role of the public in health care rationing. *Critical Public Health*, **4**: 49–54.

16 Mooney G. (1994) *Key Issues in Health Economics*, pp. 33–40. Harvester, London.

17 Drummond M. (1994) Output measurement for resource allocation decisions in health care. In McGuire A, Fenn P, Mayhew K (eds). *Providing Health Care*, pp. 99–119. Oxford University Press, Oxford.

18 Winslow G. (1982) *Triage and Justice*, pp. 87–110. University of California Press, Berkeley, CA.

The strengths and limitations of programme budgeting

Tony Lockett, James Raftery and John Richards

Introduction

The recent enthusiasm for programme budgeting (PB) among health economists would be less disquieting if these new-found converts showed any awareness of the history of the technique, all the more so given the highly unfavourable judgements that have been made about programme budgeting in the 1970s after its rise to prominence in public policy evaluation in the 1960s, particularly in the USA.

Programme budgeting appears to have been reborn free from these defects in a few pages towards the end of Gavin Mooney's book *Economics, Medicine and Health Care*[1] and expanded slightly in a 1992 NAHAT publication[2]. This modification of the approach is later referred to as PBMA.

The present paper argues that an awareness of the history of PB can help bring out both the complexity of the task and the kinds of information needed to support it. We report a case study on the use of programme budgeting for resource allocation of health care expenditure in Southampton and South West Hampshire Health Commission. The paper discusses the successes and failings of the foray into programme budgeting and explores how the approach should be modified if it is to be successful.

History of programme budgeting

PB or, to give it its full title, planning programme budgeting systems (PPBS) came out of attempts to apply systems theory to public policies, notably by the RAND corporation in relation to the siting of US military bases in the late 1950s[3]. The approach was generalized by President Johnson in 1965, who announced that all federal agency heads were to introduce 'a very new and revolutionary system' – PPBS. The new approach involved four main items: first, identify objectives; second, define time horizons; third, develop indicators of programme efficiency; and, fourth, develop and compare alternative means (programmes for) of achieving the objectives. Or in more colloquial language: 'What do we do?', 'Why are we doing it?' and 'How are we doing it?' In order to achieve these objectives PPBS sets out an approach to decision making. This approach can be summarized as:

- agree a programme format
- undertake a programme analysis examining the resource use by programme
- collate information and report the findings to aid decision making.

Programme format involves the identification of organizational objectives and the description of programmes to achieve these objectives.

This necessitates the consideration of choice and alternatives and the description in detail of the organization's mission. Analysis involves the description of the costs and benefits associated with the alternatives generated in relation to the objectives described.

The methods used may be either economic or business orientated, but whatever the methods used explicitness is the key. The final step is the collation of information into a workable package for presentation to the decision-makers. The decision-makers then make their choice and the programmes are instituted.

Given the requirement on federal agencies to undertake these tasks, PPBS spread fast. However, a highly critical review of these attempts in 1975 concluded 'We have not been able to find a single successful example of PPBS at work. PPBS has failed everywhere and at all times. PPBS is not cost effective'[4]. Wildavsky cited three categories of evidence; examples of implementation of PPBS in name only, examples of PPBS being operative but to no effect, and those where it made a difference but of unknown kind and magnitude. He concluded that the US experience played out the cycle of early enthusiasm, wide diffusion and later disillusion. Problems identified by Wildavsky (page 326) with PPBS included:

- lack of principles for defining programmes

- difficulty in linking inputs to outputs in public services

- lack of a single rationality which could be used for decision making

- omission of politics

- decision making is incremental.

Brown and Jackson[5], in one of the mainstream UK books on public sector economics with a section on PPBS, head that section which deals with PB somewhat despairingly as 'PPBS, ZBB, PAR and all that'. They see cost–benefit analysis (CBA) as one among a number of techniques (among which they include PPBS and zero-based budgeting, or ZBB) that aim to increase rationality. PPBS, they suggest, failed because of the difficulties of linking inputs to outputs and because of the bureaucratic resistance to approaches which cut across departments. They criticize Wildavsky on the grounds that:

- economists do not expect decision-makers to be rational but rather show how they might be

- economists are happy to leave politics out

- incremental decision making may be rational.

None of the other main stream textbooks even devote a section to PPBS. A global perspective on PPBS is provided by Premchard[6] in an IMF review which noted that 'the implementation of PPBS in the US government, notwithstanding the political commitment, did not deliver the revolution it promised' (p. 332). Its demise was followed by a rise of management by objective (MBO) with an emphasis on managerialism as opposed to the economic and financial emphasis of PPBS. The focus of MBO was narrow and to do with technical efficiency (producing the same services at lower cost). Allocative efficiency (producing a different, more cost-effective mix of services), which was the aim of PPBS, was incidental to MBO.

A more wide-ranging review is provided by Schick[7], who argues that budgeting is a developing process moving from immature to mature systems. Schick identifies three functions as critical to system maintenance: control, management and planning. Control was historically the first, followed by management and then planning.

After the experiments with planning via PPBS, Schick shows that national governments, especially in the OECD, have moved back to reassert control and management at the expense of planning. The UK sector has been through a prolonged period of MBO with great emphasis on control and management[8]. There are a few signs that we are moving in to a planning stage – but that of course could change.

PBMA

Mooney et al.[2] have advocated PBMA as a means for health authorities to improve allocative efficiency with a focus on the margin. They suggest eight practical steps as follows:

- define programmes
- establish programme management groups
- define subprogrammes
- focus on the margin
- draw up in/decremental wish lists
- cost wish lists

- examine the relative benefits of changes in spending

- choose.

While this is clear, the authors' suggestion that it is 'not complicated' is more questionable. Many issues are not dealt with, such as:

- how the programmes are defined

- who constitutes the programme groups ('precisely who should staff them is for the health authority to decide but they will be people well placed to form judgements about the impact of various policy changes on the programme', p. 19[2])

- how they draw up the wish lists

- how to establish the (marginal) benefits and the costs of marginal changes in expenditure.

As discussed above, these are problems familiar in the history of PPBS. Two major assumptions are made: one to do with technical efficiency and the other with information. PPBS historically has emphasized allocative efficiency and assumed technical efficiency. However, to assume technical efficiency in health services is naive, particularly given the rapid pace of technical change, the considerable variations that exist in levels of service use and costs and the lack of incentives to be efficient.

By contrast with PPBS, PBMA is almost entirely information free. No suggestion is made of use of routine data on service use which could indicate whether a purchaser is buying a lot or a little of a particular service relative to other purchasers. Since the law of diminishing returns presumably applies to many treatments, the likely health gain from marginal changes may well depend on how much one is already purchasing.

The same is true of costs given the high proportion of fixed costs in health services with the consequent low marginal costs. Spending a fixed amount may well generate different amounts of activity depending on where and how it is spent. Since marginal costs can be as low as 10% of the average cost in acute hospitals, this may matter enormously.

The emphasis on marginal analysis in PBMA requires information that is not likely to be available. The effect of this is to rely on local subjective judgements, which can all too easily reflect interest groups. If local judgements are to be relied upon, close attention to the most appropriate methodologies for eliciting preferences are required as well as ensuring that the knock-on effects of changes are understood.

These issues are returned to in the section below dealing with how Southampton plans to take PB forward.

The development of a programme budget for Southampton and South West Hampshire Health Commission

In 1994, Southampton and South West Hampshire Health Commission set about the task of developing an overall health strategy to the year 2000, described elsewhere in this book. The strategy was to set health improvement targets and to cover the use of NHS resources across the primary care, hospital and community health services. In view of the need to examine expenditure and relate it to operational and strategic goals, it was decided to investigate the use of a programme budget structure to facilitate decision making.

Programme format
The choice of programme format would be crucial to the success of the approach. There were two choices, a care group approach or a disease-based approach. The care group approach offers the advantage that the categories used, such as elderly care and children, may be the traditional 'priority services'. It also has the advantage that community care services and social services expenditure is often grouped along the same lines.

The disadvantage is that a care group approach gives no indication of spending by diseases, and it becomes difficult to prioritize services according to health needs, as the commission's strategic role demands. On the other hand, disease-based programmes have the advantage that they offer mutually exclusive categories, are amenable to epidemiological analysis and the information to support the structure is readily available from the contract minimum data set. After discussion in the commission, a disease-based approach was decided on, but one which was flexible to include a programme of expenditure representing more generic investments. The programmes may be 'flipped over' into specialties, providers or any of the relevant parameters. The programme format is shown in Table 4.2. The structure of the disease

Table 4.2 Programme categories and units

Category	Unit
1 Injury	**1** Trauma **2** Burns **3** Poisoning **4** Other injury
2 Mental health	**1** Mental illness **2** Learning disability
3 Cancer	**1** Lung cancer and other respiratory cancers **2** Cancers of connective tissue, skin and breast **3** Cancers of genitourinary system **4** Cancers of digestive system **5** Other malignant disease **6** Non-malignant disease
4 Circulatory disease	**1** Heart disease **2** Cerebrovascular disease (stroke) **3** Other vascular disease
5 Mobility and the senses	**1** Nervous system diseases **2** Diseases of sense organs **3** Musculoskeletal disease
6 Infection and internal disease	**1** Infectious disease **2** Endocrine, metabolic and immune disorders **3** Blood disorders **4** Respiratory disease **5** Digestive disorders **6** Genitourinary disease **7** Unspecified symptoms and illness
7 Pregnancy and the newborn	**1** Fertility **2** Pregnancy and childbirth **3** The newborn
8 Other health programmes	**1** Supportive and social care **2** Healthy lifestyle promotion **3** Child surveillance **4** Other health protection

based groups was based on the ICD9 classification. This gave a clear indication of the basis of the programme, as well as being capable of being meshed with the newer developments in contracting such as health care resource groups (HRGs). The use of ICD9 codes also permitted an analysis of activity directly from the regional routine data reporting system. The structure was selected so that it was also ICD10 compatible.

Cost and activity analysis
Once the format was decided, a cost analysis by programme area was performed. Separate analysis was done for hospital and community care. In the case of hospital care the analysis was done using the regional data collection system. The number of finished consultant episodes by specialty relating to the programme category or subcategory (defined by ICD9 primary diagnosis code) was read from the system.

These episodes were then priced at average specialty prices, obtained from the contracts. In the case of community care, expenditure was taken directly from the contracts and allocated to the programme areas as no routine data were available that enabled accurate apportionment of activity to programme area. Likewise primary care expenditure, in the form of cash limited and non-cash limited general medical services expenditure (GMS), was allocated using data obtained from the Morbidity Survey in General Practice 4 report. In the area of prescribing a more accurate apportionment of expenditure was available. PACTLINE data for GPs located in the catchment area were divided into programme areas using the British National Formulary (BNF) categories under which they were recorded.

Programme budget summary
Table 4.3 shows actual expenditure by health programme and subprogramme and the share of expenditure, from 1994–95 (i.e. 1993–94 out-turn activity at 1994–95 prices). Figures have been rounded to the nearest £100 000.

The development of a health strategy

The stated objective of Southampton Health Commission is to

Table 4.3 Expenditure by programme area 1994–95

	£ millions	Share (%)
Injury	**14.4**	6.5
Trauma	10.5	
Burns	1.6	
Poisoning	0.8	
Other	1.5	
Mental health	**33.6**	15.1
Mental illness	26.4	
Learning disability	7.2	
Cancer	**13.6**	6.1
Respiratory	1.8	
Skin and breast	1.9	
Genitourinary	2.8	
Digestive	2.1	
Other malignant	2.9	
Non-malignant	2.1	
Circulatory diseases	**23.5**	10.6
Heart disease	11.7	
Stroke	8.1	
Other vascular disease	3.7	
Mobility and the senses	**29.9**	13.4
Nervous system	3.6	
Senses	13.8	
Musculoskeletal	12.5	
Infection and internal disease	**68.0**	30.6
Infectious disease	8.1	
Endocrine	6.8	
Blood	3.0	
Respiratory	16.1	
Digestive	18.6	
Genitourinary	9.7	
Symptoms	5.7	
Pregnancy and the newborn	**18.7**	8.4
Fertility	5.4	
Continued		

Table 4.3, *continued*

	£ millions	Share (%)
The newborn	4.7	
Other health programmes	**20.7**	9.3
Supportive and social care	16.5	
Health promotion	1.2	
Child surveillance	2.3	
Other health	0.7	
Total	**222.4**	100.0
(excluding unassigned and commissioning overhead)		

'Secure better health for local people'. Given this background it becomes possible to set targets and to examine the range of activity and costs highlighted by the cost analysis. In each programme area the impact of the health problems was assessed (in terms of the numbers of deaths from the problem, local incidence and prevalence data, standardized mortality rates and estimates of the numbers of years of life lost). A range of available interventions was then assessed in terms of the effectiveness of the intervention, in terms of reducing the risk and reducing the impact and an assessment of its value for money.

The achievement of health targets was translated into a range of programme changes based on known effective interventions. In addition to stating the strategic direction of the commission, the strategy also attempted to prioritize expenditure to the year 2000. In order to do this the programmes were framed against projected expenditure to the year 2000 by extrapolating current funds. A series of programme changes were then developed by apportioning increases in funding according to:

- relative priorities of each programme
- the distance from the targets
- the availability of effective interventions
- the efficiency of resource use.

The priorities for investment were reflected in formula shares for new investment, as shown below in Box 2.

Box 2 Formula shares

Injury	0.80
Mental health	1.36
Cancer	0.80
Circulatory diseases	1.20
Mobility and the senses	1.04
Infection and internal diseases	1.04
Pregnancy and the newborn	0.88
Other health programmes	0.88

The development of a purchasing plan

Purchasing authorities are required every year to produce a purchasing plan giving five-year purchasing intentions. Although the health strategy gave a clear indication of the general direction the commission was expecting to take, it did not enter into a level of detail sufficient to enable a plan to be constructed. For the purchasing plan it was necessary to detail an investment and disinvestment strategy.

Investment strategy
Having identified the range of interventions in which the commission wanted to invest as part of the strategy, the commission had to decide how to prioritize these interventions alongside the other investment needs. In order to do this, it decided to examine the marginal costs and benefits produced from each investment option. This exercise, 'Purchasing Dilemmas 1994' is described in detail elsewhere in this book.

However, lack of information on marginal costs and benefits led to a process more akin to option appraisal benefit scoring being employed. The total financial costs of each option were identified and compared with aggregated subjective estimates of total benefits. Since many NHS personnel have some familiarity with option appraisal, it may provide a basis on which to build in the future. The role of true marginal analysis in this application is, however, decidedly equivocal, given the difficulty in obtaining reliable information about costs and benefits of all options to enable reasonable comparisons to be made. In other words, identifying just where 'the margin' lies in health care is much more problematical than implied in Mooney's framework[2].

Disinvestment strategy

In common with many other purchasing organizations, the commission had to consider a strategy for disinvestment in order to realize funds that could be redeployed into other areas. There are several options open to health authorities which wish to achieve disinvestment. These include the withdrawal from ineffective services, so-called top-slicing and looking for efficiency savings. On careful review of these options several problems were immediately evident.

If disinvestments were to be based on the withdrawal of ineffective treatments it would be difficult to define what an ineffective treatment was, how much should be withdrawn, and whether withdrawal would release marginal or average cost. On reviewing the data about known ineffective interventions such as grommets for children with glue ear, dilation and curettage (D&C) in women under 45 and asymptomatic wisdom teeth extraction, some £300 000 could potentially be withdrawn, if all activity was stopped and costs recovered at average cost. However, it has to be borne in mind that the commission has no direct control over the activity in these procedures and an intensive education and information programme would be needed to reduce referrals if chaos were not to ensue. There are also ethical problems to be considered in adopting such a strategy in that the decision to withdraw these services would be made on a utility argument, while the equity of the health care provision would be ignored. This is important as glue ear is a disease of the poorer section of the population. Withdrawal of services may worsen any equity imbalance and therefore this method of withdrawal begs the question about whether equity arguments may outweigh utility, a point about which members of the commission clearly felt some discomfort.

Withdrawal or the reduction of services on the basis of cost-effectiveness arguments also ran aground in the argument that, while studies showed some interventions as relatively ineffective on average, they were likely to be effective for some individuals.

Attempts to ration a service in this way can be seen as a challenge to the media to find the one deserving case.

The second option of a generalized top-slice is an attractive option but has the disadvantage that it is insensitive. The top-slice would involve negotiating a percentage reduction in the overall contract prices paid to providers in order to create a health investment fund – a strategy successfully pursued in some districts, notably Wandsworth. However, specialties that have demonstrated the capacity to make services more efficient may be penalized more than others – an apparent perverse effect. Instead, a sensitive top-slice may be appropriate. This involves identifying technically inefficient specialties by analysis of comparative criteria such as length of stay by procedure, utilization rates and readmission rates. This is a piece of work currently under development within the commission.

The role for programme budgeting in disinvestment is unclear. It is difficult to set objectives for withdrawing resource until the implications are more fully understood and the commission agrees a set of objectives set in terms of disinvestment. During the exercise it was impossible to draw up so-called 'death lists' of services and procedures to be scaled down owing to difficulties in defining what was actually an ineffective intervention.

The fact that the recent PES (Public Expenditure Survey) settlements had been larger than expected led some commissioners to argue that this obviated the need to consider disinvestments. Taking all these factors into account, the commission has decided to pursue savings due to increased technical efficiency rather than disinvestments. The role of the analysis of expenditure is clear in this area as it enables the major areas of expenditure to be identified and targeted.

Results

Our experience in programme budgeting has revealed several useful insights into the advantages and problems in adopting the technique. These can be summarized as follows.

The importance of deciding the programme format
If programme budgeting is to be useful then the programme format must relate to how the information is to be used. In our experience the adoption of a format of disease groups, with the flexibility of a further non-disease-specific programme, proved most valuable.

The analysis of information about activity and costs
The analysis of information about activity and costs is time-consuming and imposes costs.

Unless technology for more detailed unit costing (both average and marginal) is developed and becomes available, these problems will prove a barrier to the adoption and development of programme budgeting as a methodology. As information about the costs of services is particularly difficult to obtain, we used average costs as defined by the contract. Procedure-specific marginal costs were not obtainable. These problems were compounded by the lack of data for the accurate apportionment of primary care, both cash and non-cash limited, and community data. As the role of primary care increases and care in the community continues to grow, the lack of accurate information in these areas may prove a serious hindrance.

The lack of marginal costs also means that decision making using marginal values is not possible. For this reason we adopted the 'option appraisal' methodology we have described above.

The lack of comparative information
In seeking to answer the question about the right level of investments to make, and with the lack of marginal costs, comparative information about the numbers of patients treated and the costs of therapy would have been invaluable. However, this information was limited and therefore the exercise was limited to looking at the range of new investments as we have described.

The lack of clarity of the objectives
The commission set itself a range of objectives which revolved around improving health for its local population. These objectives have been discussed on many occasions and accepted. The initial ranked list reflected these objectives, but this list was deemed unacceptable as it did not fully reflect the imperative for the commission to deliver on nationally stated, centrally driven directives.

The lack of clarity of the objectives of commissions has been further confounded by the announcements of extension to the fundholding scheme. It appears that commissions will now have a lesser role in purchasing decision making.

Disinvestments
The lack of clear objectives and comparative information made the

decisions to be made about disinvestments difficult to discuss. Discussion is also hampered by the lack of information regarding identification of interventions held to be totally ineffective. There is a need for more national direction and comparative information to be made available.

Ways forward with PB in Southampton

The following are the main avenues being considered for future development:

- use of comparative information on the commission's hospitalization rates and occupied bed–days for the main diseases/treatments in each programme, including the effects of finished consultant episode (FCE) inflation and in-patient FCEs with a zero length of stay at specialty and subspecialty level whether at disease, procedure or HRG level

- linking of those data with the optimal levels of treatment on a population basis for those treatments

- costing of changes in activity on the basis of both changes in treatments (such as increased day case activity, better management of long-stay patients) and use of marginal costs (both for activity changes in the short run and for the effects of activity changes on average unit costs over the medium term)

- linking this analysis into any relevant costing exercises such as 'costing for contracting', using HRGs.

The use of the methods outlined above will give information about the technical efficiency of current expenditure and give indications of where efficiency savings could be made. However, it is still likely that other types of disinvestments will have to be made.

While these measures will allow greater investigation of acute care expenditure, we have not yet successfully resolved the issues within primary and community care. We are working with local GP practices to determine the drivers of workload in primary care. As many community services are currently driven through GP surgeries, the exercise of collecting the data for the GPs may give us better access to community information.

This aspect of development will have to wait until the initial data are collected and compared to existing expenditure estimates. The exercise to collect and collate primary care and community services data is likely to remain labour intensive. Decisions must be made as to whether, if programming budgeting is to develop, it should be limited to the acute services.

Conclusions

Programme budgeting may provide a useful framework for purchasers charged with spending public money to improve public health. The exercise of developing a programme budget has given us insights into the decision making processes employed by the commission and helped to clarify the criteria used in resource allocation.

There are, however, several unresolved problems with the use of a programme budget. PBMA is largely information free and relies heavily on the views of 'people well placed to form judgements about the impact of various policy changes'. By contrast, the original PPBS approach relied, perhaps unduly, on information on inputs and outputs. Our experience of PB with executive and non-executive directors suggests a great demand for more information to inform choices. Given the paucity of information on the cost-effectiveness (let alone marginal cost-effectiveness) and on the efficacy/effectiveness of particular procedures, comparative data may prove useful.

End note

An earlier version of this paper was presented at the Health Economists' Study Group at Bristol in January 1995 and the authors are grateful for the helpful comments received in discussion.

References

1 Mooney GH. (1992) *Economics, Medicine & Health Care*. Harvester Wheatsheaf, London.
2 Mooney GH, Gerrard K, Donaldson C, Farrar S. (1992) *Priority Setting in Purchasing: Some Practical Guidelines*. NAHAT, Birmingham.
3 Wohlstetter and Mann (1957) cited in 4.

4 Wildavsky A. (1975) In Haveman RH (ed.). *Rescuing Policy Analysis from PPBS in Public Expenditure and Policy Analysis*. Markham Press, California.

5 Brown CV, Jackson PM. (1990) *Public Sector Economics*, 4th edn. Basil Blackwell, Oxford.

6 Premchard A. (1983) *Government Budgeting and Expenditure Controls – Theory and Practice*. International Marketing Fund, Washington, USA.

7 Schick A. (1990) *Budgeting for Results – Developments in Five Industrial Countries*. PAP, New York.

8 Pollitt C. (1993) *Managerialism in the Public Services*. Blackwell, Oxford.

Reflections on a brief return to strategic planning

Colin Godber

As a contributor to the earlier 'Purchasing Dilemmas' exercise it was interesting to take part in this seminar, which was dealing with real choices over the district's future health investment. With clinical specialists virtually excluded from strategic planning by their position on the wrong side of the purchaser–provider split there was also a sense of coming up for air, of having the chance again to share one's knowledge of local needs and services with those now taking the decisions about them.

It was clearly important to contribute a generalist medical opinion, but also a view from a cutting edge which straddled community and hospital care, on some of the issues of health need and equity within the district. After 20 years at the least well-resourced end of the service it was also possible to bring experience of the hard choices and rationing that were now facing members of the commission.

The lack of clear information on the cost, cost-effectiveness and cost–benefit of most of the options under consideration was clearly going to leave the commission making most of its decisions on the basis of value judgements and 'guesstimates'. It was possible to add a clinical dimension to such decisions though it was obviously up to the health commission members to watch out for any signs of specialist bias. As a concerned observer of some of the new perverse incentives arising from the NHS and Community Care reforms there was also a responsibility to act as devil's advocate where these incentives seemed likely to distort the health investment process. It was also important to encourage the health commission to give proper weight to its own judgement where this conflicted with targets laid down from the centre (many of which are widely regarded as being driven by political and financial rather than health need considerations). This applied particularly in the areas of waiting lists and Patient's Charter targets and in the balance of purchasing on the health/social care interface.

An important precipitant of the NHS reforms had been the failure to control the previous provider-led overexpenditure on acute hospital care. Indeed, in his first annual report after the reforms the Director of Public Health had estimated that this had resulted in a 'two million a year under investment in community services', particularly for the mentally ill, the elderly and younger people with physical disabilities. With the shift to community care there was now obvious need for investment in community mental health services particularly in the inner city area and in more effective management of lesser degrees of psychiatric illness by the primary care team. Deficiencies in provision for the elderly and younger physically disabled had recently been masked by the offloading of much of their care to social services (a national phenomenon). However, with Hampshire's social care funding expected to drop severely with the tapering of the transitional grant, continuing investment in respite and rehabilitation services would be essential if this was not to backfire badly on the local hospital and community nursing services (not to mention clients and carers).

Within the acute sector some specialties were offering excellent services and attracting substantial contracts from outside the district. Others had built up waiting lists because increasing workload had outstripped their resources and clearly required extra investment to rectify the situation. In others the remedy for waiting lists lay more in attention to improved performance and cost-effectiveness than a need for further investment. In the absence of proper costings and with the pressure from the centre over waiting times the health commission had so far found itself having to throw money rather indiscriminately at both of these problems. This seminar offered the chance to question that process and redeploy investment more appropriately. This was again an area in which the local doctors present could offer some pointers.

In the debate in the seminar it was encouraging to see the health commission's efforts to develop and apply a fair and consistent set of criteria and weightings to the various investment projects. There was also clearly a desire to shift the emphasis towards prevention and to take local authorities along in that process. The presence of representatives of the district councils underlined progress in that partnership. The balance of health gain for individuals targeted by specific projects and the district population as a whole was well debated, probably most intensely over the question of a local IVF service (which as a result probably came closer to getting funding than it would otherwise have done).

There were many instances where better information on likely cost–benefit would have greatly facilitated the debate, though the resident health economist had done his best and the assembled experts and doctors attempted to give some sort of proxy weighting. What of course was lacking was similar information on the huge range of procedures covered by existing contracts, many of which may well have had much lower cost–benefit than the new projects under consideration. There was awareness of the danger of some projects being more likely to secure funding simply because health gain or cost–benefit information was available for them. Conversely, those in the area of chronic disability, where health gain was difficult to demonstrate, might be liable to lose out. This could be because it was small or only measurable in terms of reduction in health loss; alternatively the currency might be in benefit to carers, which is notoriously difficult to measure.

This problem was importantly counteracted by the commission members' real concern with the question of equity. Encouragingly, this concept was not restricted to equity of *access* to health care but also acknowledged the need to aim for equity in actual health *experience* and quality of life. This particularly related to the needs of those in the lowest socioeconomic groups, members of some local ethnic minorities and families looking after people with chronic physical and mental illness, who may need enhanced access and greater provision to achieve similar health gain or status. This was an important corrective to the temptation for health commissions to use the framework of the Community Care Act to offload costs on the border between health and social care. This has been particularly evident in the areas of long-term and respite care for the elderly, which has seen a huge shift from the NHS to the private nursing home sector, and less obviously in the increase in domiciliary nursing care procured through social services care management – thus redefining much of nursing as social care and frequently charging heavily for it.

Another perverse incentive would be the understandable tendency to focus primary care developments in the more affluent parts of the district to reduce 'defections' to fundholding (as opposed to the city centre, where there are fewer potential fundholders to be placated but where issues of need and quality of existing provision warrant priority attention). Ironically, since this seminar took place the directive has clearly gone out to chief executives to push more GPs into fundholding even though this means they are virtually cutting the branch they are sitting on. This certainly seems to herald the abandonment of the strategic planning process as exemplified by this seminar.

The largest perverse incentive of all, however, remains the continuing central focus on waiting list times. The extent to which these have been cut so far has of course been one of the most dramatic demonstrations of the effectiveness of the NHS reforms as measured by local implementation of central mandates and investment. This has been a testimony to the power of the purchaser–provider split and the much greater centralization of control in the new NHS (albeit probably helped by specialists substantially tightening access to their waiting lists). Debate within the seminar demonstrated the general scepticism as to the real health benefit represented by that achievement. Indeed, it was clear from the application of its own weightings that left to its own judgement the health commission would have invested very little extra money in this direction, let alone a recurring figure of nearly two million pounds from its growth money for the next five years.

This seems to underline a major flaw in the spirit and implementation of the reforms, namely that the government has not had the confidence in health authorities to allow them proper scope to select their own priorities. Had such choice and diversity been allowed health commissions could have learned from each other's 'experiments', enabling the country as a whole to move towards a consensus of good practice. At the moment, health authority purchasing is dominated by a central blueprint which only allows local judgements to operate at the margin. This is not a recipe for progress and maturation in local health commissioning. Ironically it may prove much harder to ensure such obedience at the district level when high levels of fundholding are achieved.

The health commission had more flexibility in applying its concern for equity on the border between health and social care as it affected the elderly and those with chronic disability. Here it elected to sustain the existing level of investment, notably in the provision of respite to carers and the retention of a niche of long-term care for people with severe problems associated with dementia. I applaud that not just as a provider of such services but as someone in close touch with the plight of patients and carers who have found their support from the NHS ebbing away. Particularly encouraging, too, has been the very substantial investment in the community mental health teams to reinforce what has been an area of serious underprovision within this district. Provided it is implemented sensibly, it may stand as a memorial to this strategic model of local health commissioning.

In summary, it was a privilege to be involved in these discussions, and to have the chance again to contribute to local decisions on health priorities and investment. It was encouraging to see and support the clear concern for equity and the appreciation that this had to relate not just to access but to the actual health experience of all sections of the local population. The commission did its best to make up for the lack of hard evidence on health gain and cost–benefit for many of the projects under consideration, and every effort was made to achieve a reasonable system of weightings and thus a valid ranking of their priority. It was sad then to see these priorities overridden to accommodate expensive politically driven imperatives from the centre which had rated low in terms of local health need. This has to be seen as an important part of the message from this publication.

The view from a small plane over Hampshire

Lawrence Maule

Recently I had the opportunity to fly in a six-seater plane. As we flew over Southampton and south-west Hampshire, I was struck by the similarities between flying and the task of commissioning health care for the area.

The first challenge when flying is getting into the air. This goes for health care planning too. There is much about commissioning which is very detailed and precise, and there are many issues and factors involved in reaching decisions. It can be bewildering as commissioners juggle with carefully worked out health strategies and broad statements of intent not only on the same day, but often in the same breath. There is a need to rise above much of this so that the wider picture can be seen.

Once a small plane has taken off the view becomes clearer but the ride can still be bumpy as the plane flies through turbulence. Prevailing winds can quickly put the flight off course unless the pilot corrects the trim of the plane.

Perhaps the most troublesome weather that south-west Hampshire suffers from is the intermittent and often unpredictable easterly gusts from Westminster and the Department of Health. These can threaten to push the commissioners well off course as they try to steer in a sensible direction. The strongest gusts often follow gales of publicity about particular health issues which commissions have already considered and given due weight to. The wind of political expediency may tempt them to re-evaluate the issue with bias, perhaps in an often vain attempt to find fair weather again.

As the wind continues to rock the plane the commissioners are glad that they have an experienced pilot in the captain's seat who has seen it all before and knows not only how to correct for such vagaries in the weather, but also how to take advantage of them so as to make the journey more pleasant and profitable in the long run.

As commissioners look down on the area they are responsible for they can continue to be buffeted by different things, such as how to weight health gain as opposed to equity, short waiting times and quality. It is important that such exercises are undertaken and decisions are reached, and while commissioners continue to feel the effects of turbulence they must be determined to stay on course and look at the overall health needs of the area so that the panorama of health provision is more balanced following their review exercise than it was before.

As we flew over one of the New Forest villages we were able to pick out a new development going up. The green-field site which it occupies had been ripe for building for many years. A few streets away a bright blue tarpaulin covered a house; they are in the process of building a roof extension.

As the commissioners scan the breadth of health care they look upon a service which has grown and developed over many years. All are agreed that much of what is offered as health care is not only valuable but valid as far as meeting an identified need of the population. Commissions look upon what is being done and alongside the reality visualize what *should* be being done. They have a responsibility to ensure that the provision of health care 'hangs together as a piece', that there is much variety but little variability in quality or access. As purchasing becomes more parochial the role of the commissioners as visionaries will become more important if we are not to see a Health Service becoming myopic and fractured. For general practitioners are not expected to take a district-wide view as purchasers. They simply climb onto the roof of their surgeries, see what is needed, and purchase what is necessary to give their neighbourhood the best health care. If consistency across a district is to be maintained then a district-wide view must be taken, and taken into consideration. As commissioners look at the situation they are aware that there are some obvious and important priorities that need to be put on the map. Other areas of disinvestment may be harder to see initially, but when identified they must be approached with the same boldness and determination as new ventures.

There are many areas of debate in health care which should not concern the intrepid 'flying' commissioner. Details about service reviews and so on should be dealt with through the contracting service except when the redevelopment is so major as to take on wider strategic importance. Minor adjustments to existing services should be dealt with through the contracting process. If services need some extension or reorganization these can be encouraged through contracting. Such matters should not be allowed to cloud the wider issues being considered on this journey into strategic planning.

Continuing the flying analogy: the New Forest is an area of outstanding natural beauty. Life would be simpler for Hampshire residents if restrictions that protect the environment were lifted. But the beauty would be lost. There are many dedicated workers in health care. Such precious qualities as commitment and kindness could so easily be destroyed as commissions and trusts strive to get value for money.

As we near the end of the millennium health professionals are treating more patients. But are we caring less? Commissioners are in a unique position to influence the style as well as the content of health care. Many doctors are deeply concerned that the valued doctor–patient relationship is being replaced by the ubiquitous and unforgiving business relationship. Despite glossy magazine pictures to the contrary, the willingness of health care staff to see their role as vocational as well as professional is beginning to waver. In identifying and specifying health services, the commissioners should emphasize the need for compassion and empathy in those that provide services and ensure that subsequent contracts are so worded that it would be possible to ensure that a service was not simply processing people but caring for them. Health professionals at every level do care, but they want the framework, resources and the stability to augment their caring role and not necessarily to have its 'quality' controlled.

As we flew at 1000 feet the buffeting and banking were beginning to take their toll on those with weaker stomachs. At terra firma, the terror was over and my stomach began to settle.

Once commissioners have made decisions about how health care is to be organized in their area and how the money is going to be spent, they find themselves back on the ground and having to live with those decisions. They may feel slightly giddy and light-headed after their journey. Certainly commissioning requires courage and boldness; those with weak stomachs and no head for heights need not apply.

They will have to walk out to the plane again at some stage in the future to review the situation, for it is ever-changing. New opportunities and challenges arise and have to be responded to by further investment and occasionally disinvestment. The wider view is an essential one for the point of focus always determines outcome. There are areas of health care which seem irrelevant or impractical at this time, but which may become crucial to the future health of the area within two or three years. As the commissioners walk away from their brief sortie into the skies they must all sit down in the arrivals hall, take out their diaries and book their next trip.

Promoting equity and avoiding prejudice

Jo Ash

Introduction

Purchasing Dilemmas was an apposite title for an event which not only exposed to critical analysis some aspects of the decision-making process within the local health commission, but also exposed some of the inherent philosophical and policy contradictions in relation to the state and health care with the NHS operating under the new order for market forces.

The event's aim was to produce a consensus on prioritized options for future investment through identification and application of explicit criteria by health commission members in a rational process – drawing on stakeholder views, scrutinized by external observers and honed against 'expert' perspectives reflecting the diverse sectors of health practitioners, academics and voluntary and community groups.

Indeed, an early dilemma must surely have been whether holding such an event would generate more problems than it might solve, and as such it should be seen as a brave attempt to explore and resolve some of the competing demands and pressures in commissioning health services.

This though was more than an intellectual, theoretical exercise since the decisions reached will be implemented in the investment programme and in purchasing care and services that will directly affect local people's lives. Understanding that end reality for people is vital in terms of responsibility and accountability for decisions taken, yet proved to be often difficult to hold to the forefront in the conceptualization of the issues and multiplicity of options considered.

With such a plurality of interest and people involved in Purchasing Dilemmas, it is inevitable that participants will have left with very different levels of satisfaction with the end results and diverse understanding of how effectively the power relations within and dynamics of the process worked in meeting the stated aims. To a large extent meeting the stated aim of a consensus ranking of options depends on the convergent or divergent shift which occurred between participants' individual start positions and others, together with the sense of collective ownership of the end results. Satisfaction with this is complicated by the extent to which or to whom participants feel accountable and are obliged or able to justify their decisions and the outcomes to constituent groups or the public.

Voluntary voice

Voluntary sector input to Purchasing Dilemmas was an explicit recognition of both its advocacy and service provision roles, and the importance of voluntary organizations as partners which must be effectively engaged if the health commission is to achieve its challenging mission of securing better health for local people, since much which impacts on people's health lies outside the ambit of control of the NHS.

In this respect, Purchasing Dilemmas was a further example of a most welcome ongoing process in which the health commission is trying to build an alliance with a wide range of stakeholders to develop its broad health strategy and to secure support, which brings complementary effort and resources alongside those available and allocated directly by the health commission to meet common aims.

Voluntary organizations in this area have consistently expressed the view, individually and through specialist forums or networks, that effective decision making about public services using public funds should be based on principles of equality of opportunity and promotion of social justice through a clear and open process including time and resources for consultation and participation; explicit criteria and parameters for changes; identifiable decision makers; public accountability with honest feedback and responsibility taken for decisions.

As Director of Southampton Council of Community Service, an umbrella organization and development agency for the local voluntary sector, my participation was requested to reflect a broad overview of the diverse interests and concerns of voluntary or community groups and the people with or for whom they work. My 'expert' perspective was drawn from both my academic background in state policy together with my knowledge of the local voluntary sector and experience of the need to listen hard to and amplify the relatively small voices of those groups and individuals who are most disadvantaged in our communities.

If minority groups are not to become increasingly marginalized or their needs ignored, then decision-makers must do more than just respond to clear majorities, articulate lobbies or powerful vested interests and must take positive action to target areas for change and allocate resources in a way which does not replicate inequality or perpetuate discrimination.

Equity versus utility

Whether the expressed aim is to secure better health for people as individuals or collectively, it is clear that existing health inequalities must be addressed in taking decisions about how and where to direct resources in future commissioning of services.

Universal resource distribution and equal spending across the population which is not targeted at existing service deficits or barriers to access will only serve to replicate historic health inequalities.

Inequalities in health do not of course equate simply with inequalities in health care. Improving availability and uptake of current health care and treatment services through more comprehensive coverage across the district would still only partially redress inequalities in health which arise from structural socio-economic and environmental determinants, e.g. social class, poverty and housing, together with individual factors such as personal lifestyle, biology or heredity.

The dilemma for the health commission in determining its investment programme and purchasing strategy is to what extent it should take positive action to counter health inequalities, and how realistically could it affect the myriad of determining factors, either unilaterally or in joint commissioning with other agencies, in order to secure health gain.

With finite resources and infinite demands at the macro level, resolution of the conundrum necessitates taking decisions which aim to maximize use of public monies for optimal public benefit by striking an overall balance between NHS-organized services providing none for some, some for all or all for some.

These decisions are based on juxtaposing the factors of efficiency, effectiveness and equity in resource allocations based on implicit or explicit, and often incomplete, knowledge and information about the efficacy of particular health interventions, treatments, prevention or care by appointed health commission members who exercise purchasing power on behalf of the local population.

Population-wide health purchasing parallels the exercise of individual consumer choice in as much as the overall satisfaction of needs or wants (whether expressed as demand or not) is determined as much by what is not chosen and why, as by what is purchased. The difference though lies in who is exercising power over whom and whose needs are or are not met and why.

In the move towards application of *laissez faire* principles to the essentially interventionist market of socialized medicine within the NHS, with surrogate purchasers rather than direct consumer spending power, it is essential to recognize the potential for both institutional discrimination and personal preferences or prejudices to cloud judgements and bias decisions on who is included or excluded from state-organized health care.

In this respect neither the apparatus of state intervention in health care nor the participants through which policy is determined and enacted can be seen as necessarily benign or neutral, since organized health care variously represents a source of career, investment opportunities and social control as well as altruistic humanitarian care. The Purchasing Dilemmas exercise must therefore be seen in the context of the processes and institutions through which the plurality of interests operate in a highly complex matrix interrelating considerations of individual liberties, democratic processes, distributional matters and social justice to determine who gets what, when, how and why.

It is therefore incumbent on all involved to strive towards making explicit the basis for decisions taken on behalf of others and to challenge consciously and constantly any collusion or cosy complacency, which can occur when group composition is too similar genuinely to reflect social diversity and minority community interests, or which arises as a defensive response induced when people are swamped by their attempts to grapple with difficult principles and competing aims.

In balancing the inherent contradictions between application of the principles of equity and utility, which lie at the crux of the purchasing dilemmas proposed, this voluntary voice clearly favoured redressing existing inequality in access to health care, to establish the baseline from which redistribution or realignment of existing services, by programme budgeting or trade-offs over the competing aims and criteria, on which resource allocations for future commissioning should take place.

In this respect the health commission's role is to be seen to be responsible, through strategic intervention informed by communities' priorities and taking cognisance of deprivation indices, for establishing health services at the macro level which everyone has a right and ability to access. The management of aggregated demand on macro-level allocated resources takes place through the gate-keeping of clinicians or health practitioners at the micro level, at which individual needs are met based on clinical judgements and rationing through the referral and waiting list procedures.

Reflections of the event

With the benefit of hindsight it is possible to identify a number of areas of weakness in the Purchasing Dilemmas event which could lead to the view that it failed to meet its own initial aim or the aspirations of its various participants. This though would be a harsh and churlish judgement on an event which at least set out to widen the basis and develop rational decision making by exposing the miasma of influences and factors to scrutiny and challenge. The following critique of particular aspects of this event is therefore offered very much in the spirit of developing and refining the process.

The preparatory 'options for change' questionnaire, designed to elicit stakeholder views, was acknowledged to be flawed because of both the process by which it was administered and the complexity of its content. Consultation of this sort needs proper preparation and inclusive circulation, sufficient time (not over a short period in the summer holidays!) and a facility to differentiate and appropriately weight aggregated, individual or mandated representative views. Similarly, presentation of so large a number of options and the associated briefing or background information needs further elaboration if it is to be more sensitively handled in such a priority ranking exercise.

Definitions of terminology and concepts proved difficult to agree, and major gaps in information about effectiveness of health interventions or outcomes and a paucity of evidence about treatment/care options *vis-à-vis* (unit) costs of investment, opportunity, marginal and cost–benefit analysis, programme budgeting and technical, allocative or productive efficiency indices were evident during the days. Further work on defining economic and qualitative data needs to be done. In striving to achieve 'value for money' in spending public resources to meet needs in communities, value must be judged in economic, qualitative, moral and ethical terms.

The two-day event itself was a lively and participative affair, conducted in an exploratory spirit, with an ambitious timetabled agenda which at times lost its direction or momentum as people struggled to absorb and analyse complex data and issues.

This was perhaps best characterized by the revisiting of criteria between the first and second days, which resulted in a very significant reordering of the ranked priorities arrived at by application of the initially agreed weighting of broad 'principles' (health gain, equity, access/localness, personal responsibility and choice) by interjection of additional 'pragmatic' criteria which appear to have shifted decisions towards the more utilitarian options.

While it is possible to posit a number of reasons for this shift, it is probably more productive simply to note its effect on the final outcomes in terms of recommendations and subsequent decisions taken for inclusion in the district purchasing plans. Many of the early priorities do not appear, most notably the original first priority for a communication service aimed at reducing one of the most fundamental barriers to accessing existing services.

Since health commission members' views or priorities at the outset of the event were not recorded, any changes in their prioritization of options as a consequence of their articulation and application of more explicit criteria could not be judged. Thus, it is hard to discern the extent to which their instinctive 'gut' reactions would have led them to conclusions the same as or different to those emerging through exposure to this process, and it is therefore only possible to speculate about the causes of shifting criteria and reordering of priorities. This was a deficiency in the event which is relevant to both the accountability of participants and the perspective from which they come, as well as to using this method in the future as the basis for more rational, open decision making.

In conclusion, the Purchasing Dilemmas event achieved in part its objective in producing a prioritized set of programme options to which collectively participants had contributed and helped formulate, although perhaps inevitably some feel more satisfied with the final outcomes than others. Certainly the event was challenging and stimulating for participants – posing complex issues and inherently contradictory imperatives about which there can be no right answer, only negotiated and consensually agreed solutions. Certainly the event widened out to other stakeholders' input into locally agreed strategy and implementation. As such it should be congratulated for its innovation, applauded for its positive intention, celebrated for its partnership approach and built on in the future.

The future strategic role of commissions

John Richards and Tony Lockett

Introduction

The priority setting exercise described in this book, Purchasing Dilemmas 1994, was based on the strategic intentions of the health commission set out in its health strategy to the year 2000, published in April 1994.

The major feature of the health strategy was its adoption of a programme budget approach, linking the amount of disease in the population and the 'health needs' arising therefrom with the health care resources expended on it.

The decision to adopt this approach marked the real transformation from being a manager of services into a health commission, with a mission of 'securing better health'. The purpose of the commission could be spelled out in measurable health targets (objectives) and its performance in securing change linked directly to its deployment of resources. Instead of having financial systems measuring only contracted activity in terms of services (e.g. specialties), disease-based programme budgeting offered the potential of a strategic planning framework for major health improvement.

The health strategy also identified some other major themes.

- Firstly, the strategy placed great emphasis on population health needs: this tends to imply that decisions will be influenced by the needs of the population as a whole rather than by specific interest groups.

- Secondly, the strategy recognized the growing importance of a 'locality-sensitive' approach to commissioning, partly as a counterweight to the increasing size of 'district' populations around the country as a result of DHA mergers, and partly because of the increasing influence of small-scale purchasing in the form of GP fundholding, vigorously promoted by the government and felt to be delivering real benefits to patients in the fields of responsiveness and access.

- Thirdly, the strategy placed great emphasis on the development of specific (health problem) commissioning strategies. The commission had developed a raft of strategies (for mental health, stroke, learning disabilities, substance misuse, etc.), and would go on to tackle other areas as dictated by priorities.

The future of commissioning

At the end of 1994, therefore, the commission finds itself having discovered its purpose – 'securing better health for local people' – and with a promising framework in place for linking strategic health objectives to health expenditure: the programme budget. In marginal analysis and other techniques borrowed from microeconomics, it has the beginnings of a workable approach to priority setting allied to a maturing and constructive relationship with key stakeholders in the local community (other agencies, providers, GPs and voluntary organizations).

However, several factors make it far from clear how the commission will secure real change. This paper looks ahead to the future health care market as it develops in the light of both the growth of commissioning and the government initiative to recognize and develop the lead role of primary care in purchasing. It offers a speculative view on how the role of commissions may develop in future. The rising popularity among GPs and policy-makers of fundholding, widely expected to become the dominant force in purchasing, calls seriously into question the future role of health commissions.

Primary care-led purchasing

The benefits of locality-sensitive commissioning, of which GP fundholding is one model, are clear and have been recognized by the commission in its health strategy. Locality purchasing offers the chance to achieve:

- a more flexible response to local needs – encouraging joint working between agencies and between providers

- a more targeted response to local variation in needs – improving local needs assessment and enabling the purchasing of health services to match those needs

- increased scope for integration of health and social care – enabling closer working between primary care and social work teams in the areas where their responsibilities meet.

Fundholding is held to have greater purchasing power in challenging and changing provider practice and greater sensitivity to the needs of individual patients through the medium of GP advocacy. EL(94)79, Primary Care Led Purchasing, makes it very clear that fundholding will be significantly broadened in its scope and rolled out to many more practices over the coming years. Increasingly, purchasing power is likely to be vested in primary care through the fundholding initiative.

Whether these advantages are real or illusory, sustainable or ephemeral, is largely immaterial. It is quite possible that health commissions will, in the future, be a relatively minor player in purchasing terms. Fundholders and consortia of fundholders will be responsible for spending decisions in future.

One suggestion is that fundholders may form mini-commissions responsible for the needs assessment and contracting of services. While this has the advantage of continuity with existing models of service, the transaction costs of such models may prove unsustainable. A possible solution to the problem of transaction costs may lie in the outsourcing of business management of fundholding.

This is an approach already seen in the USA, where pharmacy benefit management (PBM) and managed care are commonplace. These changes, which would involve GPs placing contracts with external agents, would represent a significant change in the philosophy of a service traditionally centred on public funds. The outsourcing of services would also not solve the problem of services for which GPs act as both a purchaser and provider, for example minor surgery. These services will take on a new significance in the face of total fundholding and will require careful management.

An allied approach is seen in the network and mixed models of health care maintenance organizations (HMO). Both of these models rely on a mixture of salaried physicians working for purchasers and an external network of providers contracted to provide services, often via a PBM-like organization. This model has considerable scope for development, and it is significant that HMOs are opening their doors already in the UK.

The existence of alternative models for purchasing has profound effects for health commissions. Commissions must face up to and shape their new role. Yet in doing so it will be important to retain the good features of DHAs as purchasers.

A strategic role

What will the future role of commissions be in such a market? EL(94)79 defines a 'strategic' role for commissions, but little is known of the characteristics of this role or the network of relationships needed to make it work.

Agents of change

Defenders of centralized, DHA-style purchasing cite a track record of delivering government policies. The reduction in waiting times for elective hospital procedures and the achievement of Patient's Charter standards could arguably be achieved by fundholders, but closure of long-stay institutions and commissioning of replacement community services probably could not, owing to the magnitude of the structural costs involved. These major structural changes, allied to the implementation of the community care arrangements, have required both strategic influence and joint agency working, which it would be hard to imagine individual GPs working in consort to achieve. Furthermore, the accountability of health commissions to the Secretary of State, while perhaps questionable in its own right, ensures a powerful incentive for these quangos to see that government policy is implemented. No such similar accountability exists yet for fundholders.

A population perspective

Another area, referred to above, which has characterized health commissions' approach to strategy is the population-wide perspective on health needs.

If population health needs are to be better met in future, and particularly if equity of access to health services is to be improved, there may be a substantial role peculiar to commissions here. Individual GPs, even practices, are bound by their nature to be influenced primarily by the needs of their patients.

The wider perspective may require a different approach. For example, some areas of need are little known to the typical GP, such as learning disabilities. GPs therefore may not represent the best advocates of need in such areas. The commission, if it functions effectively, can gain access to a wide range of informed advice and act accordingly in developing its strategies in partnership with GP purchasers, having due regard to the needs of the population as a whole.

An information resource

Similarly, commissions can gain access to relevant information about activity, costs and quality of services, and to research about effectiveness and cost-effectiveness of interventions. Current awareness is, of course, an important part of every GP's responsibility, but it would be unreasonable to expect GPs to have time to research effectiveness in the depth necessary to formulate commissioning strategies when their first priority is to deliver appropriate health care to their patients. There is a need for a body of expertise at this strategic level of local health commissioning.

The future agenda

Given the strengths and potential of commissioning and the transfer of purchasing power to GPs as fundholders, what then for the future? One very demanding linkage to be constructed is between the needs-led strategy work of commissions and the demand-led model of purchasing represented by fundholding. The task will be to reconcile the inherent conflicts of these approaches and to maximize their benefits.

Commissions are likely to have the following roles to fulfil:

- facilitating the development of primary care as both a provider and purchaser of services
- performance management of primary care to ensure that value for money is provided
- management of strategic changes, based on health gain and equity considerations and particularly when these have major consequences for infrastructure costs
- the management of market risk to ensure an adequate range and quality of services in the interests of the wider population.

This paper deals particularly with the last two 'strategic' roles.

Managing change

Although many of the changes to services which have occurred since the reforms can be put down to factors not dependent on commissioning, the major remodelling of services in response to health need and central directives does call for exceptional skills in change management. This is particularly so when the change involves redeployment of resources across existing service boundaries (such as acute to community-based care). Similarly, shifts in the balance of expenditure *between* health programmes (e.g. maternity and mental health) require the overview of a clear strategic vision and the ability to weigh up the consequent benefits and opportunity costs.

Major strategic change, particularly when significant start-up or infrastructure costs are involved, demands the leadership of commissions through the process of strategy development and implementation.

Strategy development, along the lines of the needs-led model developed in many commissions, will need to pay closer attention in future to the early involvement of clinicians, whose ownership has been shown to be essential in securing implementation. The levers available to commissions as purchasers have been precious few, with strategy implementation dependent on a shared desire to provide a better service for patients and clients. GPs, as purchasers, will speak with much greater authority about the needs of their patients, and have shown the ability to back their judgement with shifts of resources. Carefully managed, the scope for successful implementation of strategies has never been greater.

Risk management
As the fetters of managed competition are gradually removed from purchasers, there is increasing instability in the market which needs to be managed in the interests of the community. Until the recent intermediate-tier review (Managing the New NHS), this role was undertaken by regions, but it is increasingly plain that the mantle will be assumed by commissions. Their task will be to monitor and if necessary moderate the risk to provider viability from radical shifts in purchasing, if indeed these occur. There is also the question of risk to purchasers, as with increasing devolution of purchasing responsibility to small purchasers comes the increasing difficulty of allocating an appropriate purchasing budget to cover low-volume/ high-cost procedures (such as neurosurgery or bone marrow transplants), given the potential for a small hike in the number of referrals to increase expenditure beyond manageable proportions.

The concept of risk management is relatively underdeveloped in the context of the NHS internal market. At its simplest, however, there seem to be three alternatives for commissions.

1 No change. Commissions could attempt to continue with their existing role and relationships unchanged. It is difficult to imagine them surviving in these circumstances as their deliberations would take on ever-diminishing significance and they would add little of value to the nation's health. Commissions must avoid assuming the oft-derided characteristics of the erstwhile regional health authorities – paternalistic, interventionist and removed from the real world of health care priorities.

2 Devolved risk. If commissions were required, in effect, passively to underwrite the purchasing decisions of GPs and hold contingency funds to cover emergencies, there would be a powerful incentive for them to stifle innovation and promote reactionary policies.

3 Shared risk. In return for providing 'insurance' to small purchasers, the commission might expect some reciprocal arrangement,

such as the commitment by fundholders of their savings to help fund shared strategic changes of recognized value.

The third option has a number of advantages, representing a mutually beneficial arrangement between the commission, concerned with achieving major strategic changes in response to population health needs, and fundholders, wanting to secure services which are better suited to the demands of their patients. Such a shared approach might be based on the notion of a relational contract, recognizing that both parties have resources or knowledge that the other party needs. For example:

- Commissions possess the information systems and knowledge on which to base purchasing decisions and have skills in financial management and epidemiology. They also may have financial resources with which to insure the risk to small purchasers.

- Fundholders have professional knowledge and direct experience of patient preferences, giving them a strong voice as advocates and real leverage over providers (particularly as they control the decision to refer).

So, in return for commitment to needs-led strategies in the form of their purchasing decisions, and within parameters agreed by both parties, fundholders would receive the information they need to purchase and be insured against the financial risk of their purchasing decisions.

Conclusions

Health commissions have come a long way in the last four years, but are faced with an uncertain and demanding future. It is essential that they develop into their strategic role successfully, freed from the burden of contracting perhaps, but facing the twin challenges of change management and risk management. Their strategic role is at the heart of the purpose of the NHS, as champions of health improvement and equitable access to services. In future, their performance will be judged against their success in securing real shifts in health status where appropriate, and shifts in expenditure between and within health programmes.

When the elephants fight, it is the grass which suffers

Nick Allen and Peter Lees

A dilemma has been apparent since the beginning of the NHS in 1948, namely that the Health Service could always spend more money than it receives. In terms of the latest reforms, this translates to providers being willing and able to undertake more activity than purchasers can afford to pay for. The new roles of purchaser and provider have led to conflicting cultures, the recognition of which is key to the future of the internal market. Purchasers are held responsible, within a finite resource, for securing the best health care for a defined population with various and conflicting needs which may lead naturally to greater emphasis upon rationalizing and improving rather than progressing into new and often untested areas of clinical development. By contrast, the clinically led culture of the provider is to develop and expand; historically, there has been little incentive and minimal investment to evaluate current practice. Clinicians feel a sense of responsibility to individual patients or at most their own specialty; they cannot (and perhaps should not) have primary concern for populations about which they have no information. Faced with direct patient contact, many still feel that resources should be infinite, and cost-effectiveness arguments are often viewed with distaste. Finally, a caring approach and hard work are still equated to clinical effectiveness by many, and therefore efforts to question the latter not surprisingly often lead to anger and indignation.

Although various efforts have been made to develop ways of managing the gap between potential capacity and funding, these have usually been of a short-term nature, designed to handle financial crises and leading to no long-term solutions. The reforms which were introduced in 1991 represent a country-wide attempt to harness the power of both competition and an internal market in addressing the dilemma. However, although valuable mechanisms in many ways, competition between providers and contract negotiations between purchaser and provider can lead to decreasing collaboration between the different parts of the NHS. The additional activity achieved by the reforms is often quoted as demonstrating the greater efficiency generated by competition and the internal market. However, any such advantage can be quickly neutralized if lack of collaboration leads to the fragmentation of the services and a disregard for the views of those running them. If too great an emphasis is placed on either collaboration or the market, the annual pattern of actual and potential provider activity continuing to exceed the purchaser's ability to pay, resulting in purchaser–provider overspends or sudden cessations of work, will continue unabated. The ultimate sufferer will be the health of the population.

What is needed is a rational and strategic approach that attempts to prevent the mismatches between funding and activity rather than waiting until the mismatch occurs. Such an approach should aim to ensure that the services provided can be afforded, and that these are the services which bring the greatest benefit to the commission's residents. Few could argue with the logic of this approach, but implicit within it is the potential need for disinvestment in those services which offer least benefit. Clinicians fear disinvestment, and few have any experience of its impact; this fear, even if unfounded, is very real and must be recognized and handled well or obstruction will obscure the contracting process to detriment of all, not least the patients. The acute sector is already uneasy at the widely proclaimed political intent to move resources from secondary to primary care which seems to have little regard for the rising casemix and emergency pressures within that care sector.

The commission is charged with purchasing services for its residents according to their health needs. The contracts which it places with providers explicitly link activity and funding and therefore potentially make apparent what services are being forgone because the funding is not available. There is thus a great onus on the commission being able to justify its decisions regarding the investment of resources. To dis-charge this responsibility, a great deal of information is required, such as:

- the impact of various health problems on the community, in terms of the numbers affected and the severity of the consequences to the individual of having the health problem

- the effectiveness and costs of different preventative and therapeutic interventions, and the best way in which services should be modelled to deliver these interventions

- how well the services of current providers match the best that are possible within a given amount of resource.

Occasionally, there may be sufficient valid quantified information relating to these areas to provide the basis on which the commission can make its decisions where to invest its limited resources. Far more often, the evidence is incomplete and contradictory and many years of research would be required to provide sufficient evidence on which decisions could confidently be based. In the absence of such hard theoretical information, the commission has two options. Firstly, it can defer decision until the evidence is complete, although this is often not possible in practice; secondly, it can attempt to supplement the available evidence with expert opinion based on the training and experience of health professionals. Although not demonstrably as valid as properly collected research information, such opinion can be invaluable, particularly where there is considerable consensus.

However, the responsibility for making the decisions which so often need to be based on such expert health professional advice rests with the commission. The commission actually employs very few health professionals, most working for providers or as independent contractors. Because of the competitive and adversarial nature of the internal market, there is often resistance to seeking advice from the health professionals employed by local providers; conversely, they may be equally reluctant to give it. But collaborating with local experts can have major advantages in terms of ease of contact and rapidity of response and, most importantly, from knowing individuals sufficiently well to know from whom the best and most objective advice can probably be obtained.

Achievement of the aim of ensuring that the services provided are not only affordable but also maximize benefits to patients is unlikely unless purchasers and providers work together in these areas of common interest. The progress of medicine must not be stifled by the fear of cost containment but, equally, clinicians must face the responsibility of proving appropriateness, clinical effectiveness and cost-effectiveness. Furthermore, joint effort is needed to identify how existing resources can be deployed within providers to the greatest overall benefit to the local population.

The current process for planning and developing services is often unsatisfactory and should involve collaboration from the outset, rather than consultation only on completion. It is to be hoped this process may also serve to recognize 'creeping developments' which are the reality of everyday clinical practice and for which no satisfactory mechanism currently exists, either to fund them appropriately or to ensure they are not introduced at the expense of other well-proven developments.

It is of increasing importance to recognize and address the administrative demands of contracting and reach some form of compromise. Transaction costs are rising with the increasing complexity of the process and could easily outstrip the benefits. The key elements responsible are threefold: the rising number of purchasers with the growth of GP fundholding, the greater variation in contract design demanded (and now 'supportable' through enhanced information technology) and the lack of an agreement between health commissions and GP fundholders for a common contracting 'currency' (measurement of work). The burden for this increasing complexity falls heavily upon providers and competes directly with patient care. There is a pressing need, probably at a local level, for purchasers to adopt some level of consensus in the approach to contracting, although guidance on currency should be provided centrally. In any accord, consideration should be given to the level of enquiry within individual contract performance; this is especially relevant to GP fundholders, whose individual contracts are often relatively small, such that querying individual patient treatments may be pertinent but could easily reach a scale whereby it became administratively crippling to large provider organizations.

Financial and contracting measures may make a significant contribution to narrowing the gap between potential activity and funding, by improving efficiency. Purchasing strategy and service planning work may rationalize investment and achieve better targeting of resources on those areas that confer the greatest health benefit. There are a number of interrelated approaches that could contribute to the rationalization of clinical practice, such as:

- mechanisms for assessing the costs and benefits of medical developments in a rigorous manner

- reviewing current clinical practice to ensure that the available resources are being targeted at those activities that bring the greatest patient benefit

- developing referral guidelines covering out-patient and direct access services to ensure the appropriate use of these facilities

- reviewing the criteria that are used to determine additions to elective waiting lists

- developing management guidelines for certain health problems to identify the most appropriate balance of different professional inputs between primary and secondary care

- scrutinizing those activities which consume the most resources, by virtue of either the high volume or the high unit cost of such activity

- identifying new models of care that provide at least the same levels of quality and outcome for lower cost.

The commission has a tradition of good relationships with local health professionals in both primary and secondary care sectors, and this has been used to advantage in developing a number of the above approaches in a collaborative fashion. However, for this to be developed to the full, the issue of clinical involvement in purchaser–provider negotiations needs to be addressed and the difficulties recognized; differing solutions will inevitably be appropriate according to the circumstances, but the inescapable prerequisites are investment in protected time and peer group recognition of the importance and, indeed, respectability of clinician involvement in management.

The reforms, by breaking management links between the commission and provider units, could potentially jeopardize the advantages that the previous close working brought, particularly if there is injudicious adherence to largely outmoded models of commercial practice. The early years of the reforms were indeed marked by the encouragement of adversarial purchaser–provider relationships of a kind that would be deemed badly out of date in the commercial world. Recently, however, there appears to have been a recognition that the notion of free market competition is much less applicable to the NHS than previously postulated. Nevertheless, it is important that the advantages conferred by the purchaser–provider separation are not lost. The commission must continue to collaborate with providers to harness local professional expertise without relinquishing its responsibility for determining the pattern of health care in the area, jeopardizing the exercise of professional judgement or suppressing provider innovation. This is a tall order but, if collaboration is based on mutual respect, the identification of areas of common interest, and a willingness to understand the viewpoints of the other side, then the challenge can be met to the consequent benefit of purchaser, provider and, most importantly, the local population.

Reflections of the non-executive members

Jack Howell, Irene Candy, Brian Burdekin, Brian Irish, Bob Lee and Brian Strevens

This was a valuable exercise which involved the non-executive members (NEMs) more directly than previously in strategic decisions of the commission and did much to illuminate our roles.

NEMs are drawn from a wide range of backgrounds in order to provide the commission with a spectrum of experience and viewpoints. Some members may have wide experience of financial or strategic management at a senior level, while others may have more experience of social or community issues. NEMs bring a broad perspective to the work of the commission, which for executive members, may be clouded by their close, direct responsibility for day-to-day management issues. The role and duties of NEMs can be generally described under two headings.

I As board members:

- to be accountable to the Secretary of State and to the public for the work of the commission

- together with the executive members, as the board of the commission, to consider relevant information from all sources, and to contribute to the preparation and agreement of the overall strategy and policy decisions of the commission

- together with the executive members, as the board of the commission, to consider and agree on the availability and use of resources to implement the strategy in the form of medium- and short-term purchasing plans.

2 As an individual NEM:

- to monitor the activities of the commission and to call the executive to account for the implementation of agreed policy

- to be responsible for ensuring that measures for the correction of any deficiencies are agreed and implemented.

In decisions relating to the health strategy and purchasing plans, NEMs have equal responsibilities to other members of the commission. Each has personal and direct opportunities to influence the way in which resources are allocated to meet the health and health care needs of the local community.

Yet NEMs often do not feel equally competent to discharge these responsibilities because they are aware that they have less detailed information and knowledge about many aspects of the commission's activities than executive members. This is inevitable, given that they are not involved in direct management issues and spend only limited time on the affairs of the commission, even though this may be many times more than the 20 days per annum suggested.

It is the duty of the chief executive to ensure that NEMs are provided with adequate information to enable them to function. Unless NEMs are adequately informed they may not be aware of additional information which they should be seeking. NEMs should feel reasonably well informed, and able to request more information if required to make decisions on matters which are put to them.

Identification of options

An important issue is whether NEMs should expect to initiate the identification of options, or whether they should mainly be considering options presented by the executive for decision. Defining options frequently requires considerable background and detailed information which is not normally possessed by NEMs. If a NEM possesses such information, all well and good, but it cannot be a requirement of the NEM to acquaint him or herself with this level of detailed information. However, some options do not require any special information, merely, for example, sensitivity to the needs of the community.

Preparation of the commission's health strategy requires a great deal of detailed information and expertise and for this reason, options for the strategy are largely identified by executive members. But it is the responsibility of the whole commission to consider these (and other options if necessary) and agree on the preferred option. Of course, the commission may reject the options presented and request the preparation of further options.

Similar issues arise in preparing the purchasing plan as we saw during the Purchasing Dilemmas exercise; agreeing priorities is unequivocally the responsibility of the whole commission.

The 'Purchasing Dilemmas' exercise

Preparation of the commission's health strategy up to the year 2000 was a major undertaking which occupied several months of analysis and discussion in the early months of 1994. Two NEMs and all of the executive members had undertaken this preparatory work for further discussion and final agreement by the commission.

Given the limited time available for the Purchasing Dilemmas exercise, it was important that the health strategy had already been prepared because this identified in a detailed and considered way the most desirable developments (options) likely to be possible in the coming quinquennium.

To a large extent, the preparation of the purchasing plan is an exercise in placing the identified developments, the options, in ranking order. It is also an opportunity to revise views on the appropriateness of certain options. The commission having agreed the relative priorities, the executive can then make detailed recommendations about implementation of the purchasing plan in the light of practical issues such as the availability of resources, relationship to other activities, etc.

In essence, the health strategy defines what the commission would like to do; the purchasing plan describes how it aims to achieve this in the prevailing circumstances.

Strategic options

The preparation of the health strategy earlier in the year identified 49 options which the commission wished to achieve and believed could be achieved, given the meeting of reasonable expectations of resources, both new and those resulting from redeployment of existing resources.

We believe that it was essential that the whole commission, executives and non-executive members, should consider together, in a public forum (in the sense that representatives of the public were present as observers and proceedings were recorded for publication), the basic values which would underpin its subsequent decisions. Much of this discussion involved revisiting previous decisions of the commission which had been used, for example in the preparation of the health strategy.

Conclusions about the exercise

While there are some areas which, in the light of experience, we would consider modifying if repeating this exercise, overall we consider it to have been well prepared and very worthwhile. By involvement in this structured exercise, our decisions were more informed and focused, and therefore more defensible should they be challenged. We are aware that we can never make these decisions totally objectively and that we were often relying on 'gut feeling' in which we include our personal weightings of different factors. What we wished to ensure was that our 'gut feeling' was supported by information and knowledge.

We also feel that if members of our community examine the process we went through, they will feel more confident that the decisions were made by a group of individuals who had had the opportunity to be informed about medical, social and ethical issues and had taken into account what they knew of their wishes and preferences.

We believe that we are no different from other groups of NEMs in being uncertain from time to time about whether we are adequately discharging our roles and responsibilities. We have no doubts about our responsibility to monitor the work of the commission and that of our executive colleagues. We also know that we have a key role in deciding the strategy and the policies of the commission based upon the widest knowledge of the circumstances that should influence us in this role. But we are often uncertain whether our level of knowledge is adequate; whether we should be seeking more detailed information; whether we should be more active in some areas; or, if we were, whether we would thereby be interfering in the proper role of the executives. The role of the NEM is easy to define in general terms but more difficult to interpret in the specific.

The Purchasing Dilemmas exercise has been for us a timely exercise in one of the major roles of the NEM – deciding how resources should best be used in the interests of the local community.

We have been aware of the complexity of the processes involved but rarely have we had such an opportunity to crystallize or focus our thinking at the very time when decisions are having to be made. In fact, there has probably never been an opportunity to do so in the course of the usual activity of the commission, and a formal exercise of this type has been both informative and reassuring. We have each learned lessons and can see ways in which the process could have been improved, and no doubt these will be implemented in future exercises of this type. Many of these are described in the pages of this report and need not be repeated here.

Having been through the exercise, we know that we have been actively involved in the crucial decision making of our authority and that we have done so against the background of more explicit knowledge and information as well as the revisiting of basic values which otherwise might have remained subliminal and unqualified. We believe that many NEMs elsewhere would benefit from a formal well-prepared exercise of this type, tailored to their own circumstances. If we have any lingering uncertainty, it is whether we should have had longer to consider, discuss and decide before having to commit ourselves. We suspect that this feeling was not confined to the NEMs. But how much more time and discussion would have been needed; there comes a time of diminishing returns when 'the best becomes the enemy of the good'. In retrospect, perhaps we weren't so far out.

5 Outstanding issues

What did the Southampton experience contribute to the process of priority setting? Two factors stand out:

- the development of a health strategy which made it possible to relate needs assessment more closely to purchasing decisions
- the development of a method for ranking the criteria used in the priority setting process.

A number of issues still need to be resolved.

National direction or local discretion?

Some choices were made in response to local discretion but, otherwise, national and regional targets prevailed. This may be unreasonable, as the district is fairly 'average' in terms of the health status.

Exclusions were not chosen at Southampton but is more guidance needed from the Department of Health? Does it matter if services differ from district to district? Would the public be more receptive to rationing if it was applied on a uniform basis nationally?

How to involve stakeholders

The public finds it difficult to assign priorities to treatments and needs more information to do so. In Southampton, the public preferred to leave hard choices to the commission. What is the best way to consult the public and what account should be taken of its wishes? Should its role be confined to the solicitation of the values or criteria needed to set priorities?

Other stakeholders, especially other agencies and co-purchasers (including GPs and social services), have a very direct interest in the choice of priorities by the commission and have increasing influence over the extent to which its decisions may be implemented. It therefore makes sense to consult these stakeholders so that the commission makes informed and realistic choices. But this work is in its infancy and the methods adopted in Southampton, as elsewhere, were fairly crude.

How to involve providers

Likewise, provider wishes can influence priorities in the development of health strategies as well as in the fixing of contracts. Through the development of clinical guidelines, they can also help to identify beneficial procedures. They, too, form an important stakeholder group and were consulted in the questionnaire survey.

What other account should be taken of provider wishes, particularly of clinicians? Should they be involved in the development of criteria or the selection of priorities?

How to make better use of economic evaluation

Limited cost–utility data mean that marginal analysis techniques can seldom be employed in their purest form. QALYs were available for only 10 of 49 options in Southampton. The only cost data that could be used were the estimates of implementing the various options. Still, financial pressures in the UK are driving health authorities in the direction of looking more purposefully at cost-effectiveness. Similar forces are operating elsewhere.

The benefits of an economic way of thinking in enabling more informed decisions should not be underestimated. What can be done to set priorities more in accordance with cost-effectiveness? Will the development of clinical guidelines be sufficient to identify beneficial procedures or are other procedures needed? The section by Raftery, Lockett and Richards (*see* pages 90–106) suggests some likely avenues for further work.

Protection for the chronic sick and vulnerable groups

Efforts are being made everywhere to shift resources to the chronic sick and vulnerable groups as well as to prevention and community care. Yet outcome data are not sufficient to justify this preference, and countervailing pressures may divert priorities to the acute sector. The many perverse incentives of the managed market in health care present a formidable challenge, as discussed in Colin Godber's section (*see* page 94).

What can be done to ensure adequate provision for prevention, community care and services for patients with long-term disabilities?

How to guard against age and lifestyle discrimination

Age and lifestyle have generally been ruled out as criteria in setting priorities, but they may be considered by clinicians when assessing outcome. That is the situation at Southampton, but elsewhere in the UK, age has been a factor in determining access to renal analysis, and smokers have been denied heart operations. It is not always clear that this has been done solely on the basis of an assessment of outcome.

Should age and lifestyle *per se* be adopted as criteria for setting priorities? If not, what measures can be taken to ensure that they are only applied in an assessment of outcome? Although not considered during the Southampton exercise, these considerations are emerging as significant and controversial issues.

Further reading

Cohen D. (1994) Marginal analysis in practice: an alternative to needs assessment for contracting health care. *British Medical Journal*, **309**: 781–4.

Ham C, Honigsbaum F, Thompson D. (1994) *Priority Setting for Health Gain*. Department of Health, London.

Heginbotham C, Ham C, with Cochrane M, Richards J. (1992) *Purchasing Dilemmas – a Special Report from the King' Fund College and Southampton and South West Hampshire Health Authority*. King's Fund College, London.

Honigsbaum F. (1991) *Who Shall Live? Who Shall Die? – Oregon's Health Financing Proposals*. King's Fund College Papers, London.

Honigsbaum F, Calltorp J, Ham C, Holmstrom S. (1994) *Priority Setting Processes for Healthcare*. Radcliffe Medical Press, Oxford.

Appendix A Local health problems

During the development of the health strategy to the year 2000, an assessment was made of the main local health problems in terms of their 'impact' on the health of the population. Some *29* problems were selected for particular attention in the strategy because they are major causes of mortality (death) or morbidity (illness) in absolute terms, or because the health of local people is poor comparatively speaking. These include the five 'Health of the Nation' key areas.

The health strategy arranges health problems into eight programmes, forming the structure of the programme budget, which looks at how health resources are used across primary, secondary and community care.

This section summarizes very briefly the main characteristics of each programme and the major health problems in terms of their impact.

Programme overview: injury

This includes accident prevention; immediate and subsequent care of accident victims and long-term rehabilitation for those with head and other serious injuries. Death rates from accidents have been falling for many years but, with a faster decline in many fatal infectious diseases, accidents have emerged as the leading cause of death in younger age groups. They also cause a considerable proportion of permanent disability and much short-term illness. Deaths from accidents are strongly associated with social class. Accidents are more likely in conditions of poverty, overcrowding and poor physical environment. Alcohol is estimated to be a contributing factor in 20–30% of all accidents.

In particular, the commission has focused on:

- trauma

- poisoning.

Programme overview: mental health

This includes prevention, treatment and, where necessary, long-term care of people with psychological distress, neurotic and psychotic mental disorders, those affected by substance misuse and both presenile and senile dementia. Mental health problems are a leading cause of illness, distress and disability. Almost 40% of deaths in this programme are due to suicide.

In particular, the commission has focused on:

- dementia

- substance misuse

- suicide.

This programme also includes learning disabilities:

- There are approximately 260 children and young adults under the age of 19 with severe learning difficulties in the commission area who are known to health service agencies. Down's syndrome is the commonest single diagnosis.

- There are several hundred adults with learning disability living predominantly in the community, often without family support.

Programme overview: cancer

Although more deaths occur from circulatory disease, cancer claims a greater proportion of years of life lost. There is increasingly good evidence to show that the majority of all cancers are potentially preventable, using knowledge that is currently available.

In particular, the commission has focused on:

- breast cancer

- lung cancer

- cervical cancer

- skin cancer

- bowel cancer.

Programme overview: circulatory disease

Almost half of all deaths are due to diseases of the circulatory system, principally heart disease and stroke.

Coronary heart disease (CHD) is the single commonest cause of death in England. Although the district mortality rates are lower than the national average, it remains the main single cause of death for all ages and for those under 65 years.

Stroke is a leading cause of death and disability in the country. Most deaths (93%) occur after the age of 65. Apart from good nursing and rehabilitation, current treatments have not been shown to have a major impact on case fatality and disability. There is much greater potential for reducing the burden of stroke on the community by stroke prevention.

Programme overview : mobility and the senses

This includes diseases of the nervous system, sense organs, skin, subcutaneous tissue, musculoskeletal system and connective tissue. This programme includes some major sources of disability in the population, including vision and hearing problems and problems with mobility.

- A total of 1827 people are registered as visually impaired.

- Some 20 000 people have moderate or severe hearing loss.

- Mobility problems account for around 11% of all GP consultations.

Programme overview : infection and internal disease

This programme includes infectious and parasitic diseases, endocrine, nutritional and metabolic diseases and immunity disorders, blood disorders, diseases of the respiratory and digestive systems, genito-urinary disease, unspecified symptoms and illness.

This programme includes a major proportion of health problems which lead to elective work in hospitals – gynaecology, general surgery and general medicine. It also covers the major health problems:

- prevention of infection

- asthma

- diabetes

- HIV/AIDS

- dental disease.

Programme overview : pregnancy and the newborn

This programme includes contraception and abortion services, the investigation and management of infertility, parent education, care of all pregnant women and care of babies in the neonatal period (infants up to one month of age).

The major categories in this programme are:

- unwanted teenage pregnancy

- pregnancy and childbirth

- newborn problems.

Programme overview: other health programmes

This category includes a range of health programmes which are not specific to a particular health problem, including 'lifestyle' health promotion activity, child protection, respite and convalescent care and investment in the infrastructure of primary and secondary care.

The following topics have been selected for particular attention by the commission:

- child protection

- smoking

- exercise

- nutrition.

Appendix B Options for change and indicative costs

All costs are recurring except where noted 'NR' – non-recurring.

Health programme: injury

	Indicative cost (£000)
1.1 *Mixed crew trials*	29

1.1 *Mixed crew trials*

The Hampshire Ambulance Service are conducting a pilot exercise to evaluate the benefits of introducing two new 'mixed' crews (one qualified and one basic grade ambulance person) at the Southampton station. These crews would carry the low-dependency and many high-dependency non-urgent patients who are currently transported by first tier (fully qualified) crews.

Subject to the outcome of this (available in August 1994), the commission may be asked to pick up the additional costs of this development.

The benefits of this would be more efficient use of resources and an improved level of service across the district.

1.2 *Immediate care training: crash-call GPs*   20
Training is available to equip GPs with the necessary
skills ('BASIC') to intervene at the site of an accident,
thereby complementing the ambulance service and saving
valuable time, giving rise to better outcomes. The
commission could extend the provision of training and
support to provide more of this type of cover.

1.3 *Community first aid training*   10
Education in basic first aid and resuscitation skills for
members of the public can help to reduce mortality,
especially if targeted at relatives and carers of those at
high risk, such as people with heart problems or diabetes.

1.4 *Accident and emergency*   137.5
The Patient's Charter sets a standard that all patients   (11NR)
should be treated within one hour (following
immediate assessment).
Some further investment may be necessary to meet this
standard at Lymington, Hythe and the Eye Unit.

1.5 *Multiagency accident prevention*   27
Several agencies, including local authorities and education,
have a role to play in creating a safer environment and
reducing the risk of accidents (including accidental
poisoning). The commission may help to resource a
coordinated planning effort, resulting in a contract to
develop and implement an agreed preventative
programme targeting those at greatest risk.

1.6 *Information for accident prevention*   20
Better information is needed to inform preventative
programmes and monitor progress in this key 'Health of
the Nation' area. Much of this information is routinely
available but requires collation, analysis and dissemination.

1.7 *Loan or sale of safety aids*   10
The commission may opt to contribute to local authority   (40NR)
schemes to provide safety aids (such as stair gates, safety
helmets, etc.) to low-income families in an effort to
create a safer environment for those most at risk from
domestic accidents.

1.8 *Trauma centres*   50

This involves the introduction of separate wards and
theatre lists for trauma patients, giving rise to more
effective use of resources and improved quality in the
treatment of trauma. Separation from orthopaedic
operating lists would minimize the risks of postponement
and delay to the latter as a result of the emergency
workload. Trauma patients can be discharged in four to
seven days under these arrangements (rather than ten to
14 days in a mixed ward).

Health programme: mental health

	Indicative cost (£000)

2.1 *Community mental health teams*   1300

The joint purchasing strategy recommends the   (shared
establishment of community teams in each of five   with
localities, backed up by appropriate support services. social
This would have the benefit of improving choice   services)
by offering an alternative to hospital admission, improving
access to psychological therapies and providing a more
local service in response to user preferences. The aim is
to improve the health and social functioning of people
with mental health problems.

2.2 *Locally based hospital units (LBHUs)*   900

The ultimate aim is to replace LBHUs with appropriate
community-based residential care for people with
learning disabilities. However, in the interim, there is a
pressing need for improvements to the physical
environment and services in these ageing facilities to
maintain and enhance the quality of care provided.

2.3 *Home and day detoxification*   100

The joint substance misuse strategy recommends the
establishment of five locally based teams to provide home/
day detoxification and treatment. This would be balanced
in the medium term by a scaling-down of residential

services, but would initially provide 200 detoxifications
and 1000 additional client contracts annually. This
development will yield benefits in terms of improved
referral opportunities and a greater choice of settings in
response to user preferences.

2.4   *Brief interventions*   2
The substance misuse strategy also recommends a
programme of 'training for trainers' in identification of
problem drinkers and provision of brief counselling/
advice. This has been shown to be an effective low-cost
intervention in reducing the number of people drinking
at levels likely to cause them harm.

2.5   *Substance misuse education*   40
The strategy also recommends contracting for a teacher/
adviser in substance misuse to develop school policies and
train teaching staff. The aim is to provide young people
with the skills to avoid drug and alcohol misuse.

2.6   *Improved information and support for carers*   10
The increasing burden of ill-health among the elderly and
long-term mentally ill places considerable demands on
carers, together with the effects of shorter hospital stays
and community-based services. Carers (e.g. families)
require better access to information about services,
respite arrangements and support groups.

2.7   *Increased respite and day care*   400
This recommendation of the joint mental health strategy
involves the increased provision of non-residential support
services in the form of social and therapeutic day services,
especially in the evenings and at weekends, together with
respite care, relieving the pressure on carers. This would
assist long-term rehabilitation and help to reduce total
disability and deterioration in social functioning.

2.8   *Improved detection and treatment of depression in primary
care*   20
The Hampshire Depression Project aims to provide training
for GPs, practice nurses and health visitors in the
recognition and effective treatment of depression. This is
a national initiative following evaluation of the clinical

effectiveness of alternative interventions, and will result
in the reduction of suicides (a local health target) and
improved outcomes for people who are depressed.

2.9 *Counselling in primary care*   600
   There is good evidence to suggest that the provision
   of psychological counselling in a local care setting for
   those suffering from significant psychological distress is
   effective, with lower relapse rates than traditional
   alternatives, such as drug therapies. Users and GPs have
   expressed a preference for this approach, which may
   deliver some 5000 brief interventions per year with
   improved outcomes for people with mental health
   problems and reduction in suicides.

2.10 *Supported housing*   1700
   The joint mental health strategy recommends the   (shared
   increased provision of 'supported housing' to assist the   with social
   rehabilitation towards independent living of people with   services)
   mental health problems. This is part of a flexible
   approach to supported housing, residential care and
   support services which users have asked for. The service
   would range from 24-hour health and social care to
   lightly staffed group homes, all in a domestic
   environment. Some inappropriate 'crisis' admissions to
   hospital would thus be avoided.

Health programme: cancers

	Indicative cost (£000)

3.1 *Home-based palliative care*   50
   There is evidence that palliative care based in the home,
   particularly for cancer, can be effective in providing
   adequate clinical support and a more appropriate setting
   for those who are dying. User surveys indicate a
   preference for home care. An increased service better to
   meet people's needs could be provided as an 'outreach'
   facility by existing palliative care providers.

3.2 *Concentration of treatment in specialist teams*   350
A transfer of activity to specialist centres (especially for
bowel and breast cancers) would lead to improved
outcomes, in line with the recommendations of the
Department of Health policy framework (May 1993). This
change would ensure access to expertise in the management
of cancers (including diagnostic and therapeutic techniques)
and a better choice of treatment (including, for example,
breast conservation and reconstruction). Reduced
mortality from breast and bowel cancer are local health
targets.

3.3 *Skin cancer prevention*   50
Advertising campaigns (e.g. 'Playing Safe in the Sun') on
TV, radio and in newspapers and in community pharmacies
during the summer months can be effective in reducing
risk behaviour and hence help in slowing the increase in
the incidence of skin cancer (a Health of the Nation and
local health target). Evidence from abroad (e.g. Australia)
indicates the effectiveness of a carefully designed and
targeted programme.

3.4 *Early recognition of skin lesions*   26
Early detection of skin cancer is a key factor in improving
outcomes as it can lead to earlier treatment. This is
possible through improved education of the public (see
paragraph 3.3) and health professionals to provide
increased awareness of and competency in identification of
skin lesions. Training could be provided (half-day) for one
GP in every practice.

Health programme: circulatory diseases

Indicative
cost
(£000)

4.1 *Cardiac rehabilitation*   50
The multiagency CHD prevention strategy recommends
commissioning a community-based rehabilitation programme
for 200 patients per year, leading to improved quality of

life and a quicker return to work for patients recovering
from heart disease. A locally based service would improve
access and help reduce mortality (a health target).

4.2 *Community stroke rehabilitation*   NIL
The stroke purchasing strategy recommends a new model (250NR)
of care based on the limitation of acute hospital care to an
average of seven days followed by discharge to locality-
related multidisciplinary rehabilitation services. This will
provide earlier access to high-quality rehabilitation in a
variety of settings, offering greater patient and carer
choice, and bringing care closer to the home. The aim is
to improve the quality of life attained by stroke patients
as well as reducing mortality. Implementation will be the
first stage towards a comprehensive stroke service, which
will also include improved arrangements for acute care.

4.3 *Targeted stroke prevention*   10
The number of strokes could be reduced by effective
preventive interventions. The stroke strategy also
recommends a planned programme of innovative stroke
prevention work, addressing risk factors in high-risk
groups, including Asians and Afro-Caribbeans.

Health programme: mobility and the senses

Indicative
cost
(£000)

5.1 *Care attendants*   Not known
Care attendants provide personal support for disabled
people, helping them to wash, dress and go out, and
collecting their shopping and so on. Such services are
normally considered beyond the scope of 'health care', but
the commission has recently funded a pilot scheme run by
Southampton Care Association. It is considering extending
this or similar schemes for the future.

5.2 *Community-based orthopaedic clinics for older people*   NIL
Following the major reorganization of orthopaedic   (100NR)

services in Southampton, the commission is now looking
at the next stage in its orthopaedic strategy, involving a
shift into community settings (practices and/or community
hospitals) of out-patient orthopaedic clinics. This will
provide care, especially post-operative follow-up, closer
to home, improving both access and choice, especially for
older people who may have greater difficulty in travelling.

5.3 *Increased knee replacements*   Not known
A Department of Health needs assessment project
recommended a target of 700 knee replacements per
million population. This translates into a target of 325 per
annum by 1997–98, taking into account the increasing
needs of an ageing population. This initiative will prevent
a rise in the length of time people have to wait and give
quicker access to assessment and admission for treatment,
thus reducing the pain experienced by people with knee
problems and improving their mobility.

5.4 *Community-based rehabilitation*   570
Many minor conditions can be treated and managed
outside major acute hospitals, thus relieving the pressure
on acute in-patient services and day surgery/day-care
facilities. This initiative involves the early discharge of
patients from acute orthopaedic facilities to community
hospitals closer to home for rehabilitation. The benefits
are easier access for patients and relatives, particularly
the elderly, and more efficient use of available resources.

5.5 *Preadmission clinics*   7
These clinics assess the suitability and preparedness of
patients for day surgery, including assessing home
circumstances which are relevant to discharge
arrangements. The commission is committed to increasing
day surgery rates, and this initiative would deliver benefits
such as fewer people unexpectedly retained overnight,
fewer people turned away on the day of their operation
and improved planning of discharge arrangements
(quicker recovery and less risk of complications – clinical
or social).

5.6 *Equipment/aids for disabled people*   150
The commission is currently reviewing the level of need
for mobility aids (from walking frames to special
mattresses) and the degree to which it is presently being
met. With earlier discharge from hospital and more
dependent people living at home, it is likely that additional
investment will be required.

5.7 *Mobile retinopathy screening*   50
The commission has recently purchased a new mobile
screening service for diabetic retinopathy, which aims to
cover those patients registered as diabetics. However,
although only 60–70% of diabetic patients are thought to
be registered, this may increase as the service becomes
more widely known. This expected increase may require
additional investment. Retinopathy screening has been
shown to be effective in enabling earlier treatment of
this disease.

Health programme: infection and internal disease

	Indicative cost (£000)

6.1 *Asthma patient education in primary care*   10
The mortality from asthma in this district has shown
little sign of improvement over the last decade and the
prevalence of the disease is increasing. There is an
indication that GPs may be underprescribing drugs which
prevent asthma (anti-inflammatories) and possibly
overprescribing drugs for the treatment of acute attacks
(bronchodilators). The health commission has set a target
to reduce the ratio of inhaled bronchodilators to anti-
inflammatories from 2:1 in 1993 to 1.5:1 by 1996. This
could be achieved through educational programmes which
lead to the improved management of asthma in primary
care.

6.2 *Sex education in schools*   32
A teacher–adviser to develop school policies and train

teachers in sex education is recommended by the joint
strategy for unwanted teenage pregnancy, leading to a
reduction in unwanted pregnancy and improved sexual
health.

6.3 *Community-based needle exchange*   (25NR)
The joint purchasing strategy for substance misuse
recommends the establishment of a pilot project based on a
large housing estate in the east of Southampton to reduce
needle sharing by injecting drug misusers and provide
better access to counselling and support for families and
carers.

6.4 *Parent/carer education in oral health*   10
Dental decay is preventable. Dietary changes are the
cornerstone of preventive action by individuals (e.g. sugar
reduction). Eighty per cent of decay occurs in 20% of
children, and a targeted approach is necessary. Parents
and carers of those children most at risk have a major
influence on their dietary habits. Further development of
the current programmes is necessary, involving
preparation of educational videos and other media.

6.5 *Targeted oral hygiene education*   10
Fifty per cent of children aged 15 have evidence of gum
inflammation (the first stage in gum disease, which is the
main cause of tooth loss in adults). This can be prevented
by correct oral hygiene. Education programmes already
cover 25% of the target 14-year-old population, and it is
proposed to extend this coverage to 50%.

Health programme: pregnancy and the newborn

	Indicative cost (£000)
7.1 *New models of maternity care*	100

7.1 *New models of maternity care*
The commission's maternity strategy recommends new
models of maternity care based around preconceptual

care, a decrease in routine antenatal visits for
uncomplicated pregnancy, outreach antenatal facilities and
continuity of midwife care before, during and after giving
birth. These models increase the choices available to
women, improve the information available to women and
improve access to a more local service.

7.2 *Unwanted teenage pregnancy: education programme/*   50
counselling and contraceptive clinics   (2.5NR)
The joint strategy for reducing unwanted teenage
pregnancy recommends the additional provision of special
advisory/counselling and contraceptive services for young
people in localities currently underserved (Hedge End,
Bitterne and New Forest), linked with a programme of
publicity to raise awareness of these services. The aim is to
improve the uptake of these services and hence reduce
unwanted pregnancies and abortions.

7.3 *Assisted conception*   1000
New techniques such as *in-vitro* fertilization offer the
only chance of having a child for some couples with
certain causes of infertility. These interventions are
currently available only to those able to pay privately.
The commission may consider funding a new service,
aiming for up to 50 babies per year by assisted conception
treatments.

7.4 *Preconceptual use of folic acid*   10
Folic acid has been shown to improve significantly the
health of infants when taken by mothers before conception,
including a reduction in neural tube defects (spina bifida).
An education programme for professionals and women
generally about the benefits of folate and appropriate
sources is required.

7.5 *Ambulance paramedic obstetric training*   25
The maternity patient's charter requires that ambulance
paramedics are competent in basic obstetric care in order
to provide emergency help and thereby contribute to
improved maternal health and reduced infant mortality.

Other health programmes

Indicative
cost
(£000)

8.1 *Waiting times and access*   1900
The commission is committed to reducing waiting times
for elective surgery, and has succeeded in achieving a
maximum 12-month wait for in-patient and day case
admissions. However, certain conditions (such as heart
bypass surgery) need much shorter maximum waiting
times, and out-patient waiting (target 13 weeks for adults
and six weeks for children) is still unacceptably long in
some specialties (e.g. ENT and orthopaedics).
Furthermore, the commission is aiming to reduce in-
patient/day case waiting further to a maximum of
nine months. Additional investment is required to achieve
these improvements in access which are linked to the
Patient's Charter and government initiatives.

8.2 *Child protection: primary care training*   10
About 400 child protection conferences are held annually
to assess children considered to be at risk of abuse. At
any time, some 170 children are on the Child Protection
Register. The commission intends with social services to
review the range and effectiveness of services currently
purchased. However, there is an apparent need for
training for GPs and primary care teams in the
recognition of and appropriate response to child abuse.

8.3 *Child protection: medical input to assessment*   20
The assessment of children who have been abused would
benefit from greater medical input. There is a need for
24-hour on-call arrangements for urgent examinations
and increased input from community child health services
and child guidance clinics.

8.4 *Smoking reduction: primary care training in motivational
interviewing*   10
Motivational interviewing is an effective approach to
smoking cessation, and this proposal involves training GPs

and primary care teams to advise 80% of smokers in each
practice population, on either an individual or a group
basis. The reduction of smoking is a health target and will
contribute to reduced mortality and morbidity from lung
cancer and heart disease.

8.5 *Dietetics: training for primary care*   25
Dietetics (or nutritional advice) can be effective in
tackling a wide range of health problems, including heart
disease. A practice-based service, working with the
primary care team, would provide patient consultations
and staff training. This service is not available currently
and would facilitate improved links with the hospital
dietetics service following discharge.

8.6 *Communication service for ethnic minority patients*   50
Many patients from the black and minority ethnic
populations are disadvantaged in accessing and using
health services owing to language barriers. This is also an
issue for professionals in diagnosing, treating and caring
for patients appropriately and effectively. An interpreting
service can help communication by providing trained and
skilled personnel for this client group using health
services.

This service will deliver many benefits, including
appropriate and responsive treatment and care; risk
reduction to both client and staff; respect for religious
and cultural aspects of care; client participation; and cost-
effectiveness.

8.7 *Domiciliary care*   100
Domiciliary care may be an alternative to hospital,
nursing home or rest home care, provided that it is
adequately resourced. Older people with varying, often
multiple, health problems require supportive care for
their chronic illnesses, and sometimes follow-up after
discharge from hospital. A range of services is required
to offer a realistic choice to users and carers. This may be
more expensive than traditional alternatives, but may give
rise to better long-term health outcomes.

Appendix C Marginal value

This section presents what is available in cost–utility analysis information about the options for change. This is intended to provide some measure of the relative efficiency (or 'value for money') of each option with reference to its utility (additional years of life, adjusted for 'quality of life').

As can be seen below, very few of the options have appraisals, and many more are not applicable to the QALY methodology.

This information is presented to inform choice and to underline the importance of other methods in priority setting.

Option	Programme/option	Cost/QALY (£)
1.1	Mixed crew trials	Not applicable
1.2	Immediate care	500
1.3	Community first aid	200
1.4	A & E	Not applicable
1.5	Multiagency prevention	Not known
1.6	Prevention information	Not known
1.7	Safety aids	Not known
1.8	Trauma centres	240
2.1	Community teams	Not known
2.2	LBHUs	Not applicable
2.3	Home/day detoxification	300
2.4	Brief interventions	Not known
2.5	Substance misuse education	Not known
2.6	Information and support for carers	Not known

Option	Programme/option	Cost/QALY (£)
2.7	Respite/day care	Not applicable
2.8	Detection and treatment of depression	1000
2.9	Counselling	300
2.10	Supported housing	Not applicable
3.1	Home-based palliative care	Not applicable
3.2	Specialist teams	Not known
3.3	Skin cancer prevention	Not known
3.4	Early recognition of skin cancer	1000
4.1	Cardiac rehabilitation	Not applicable
4.2	Stroke rehabilitation	Not applicable
4.3	Targeted stroke prevention	Not known
5.1	Care attendants	Not applicable
5.2	Community orthopaedic clinics	Not applicable
5.3	Knee replacements	1100
5.4	Community rehabilitation	Not applicable
5.5	Preadmission clinics	Not applicable
5.6	Equipment/aids	Not applicable
5.7	Mobile retinopathy screening	Not known
6.1	Asthma education	Not known
6.2	Sex education	Not applicable
6.3	Community needle exchange	Not applicable
6.4	Parent/carer oral health	Not applicable
6.5	Targeted oral hygiene	Not applicable
7.1	New maternity care	Not applicable
7.2	Education/contraceptive clinics	Not applicable
7.3	Assisted conception	Not applicable
7.4	Folic acid	Not known
7.5	Paramedic obstetrics	Not known
8.1	Waiting times/access	Not applicable
8.2	Child protection training	Not known
8.3	Child protection assessment	Not known
8.4	Smoking advice training	270
8.5	Dietetics training	270
8.6	Communication service	Not applicable
8.7	Domiciliary care	Not applicable

Appendix D Health benefits

Programme/option

Each option has been given a score of 0 to 3 in terms of the *population* health benefit it is expected to yield (0 = no additional benefit, 3 = high additional benefit).

		Health benefit
Injury		
1.1	Mixed crew trials	0
1.2	Immediate care	1
1.3	Community first aid	1
1.4	A & E	1
1.5	Multiagency prevention	2
1.6	Prevention information	1
1.7	Safety aids	1
1.8	Trauma centres	1
Mental health		
2.1	Community teams	3
2.2	LBHUs	1
2.3	Home/day detoxification	2
2.4	Brief interventions	2
2.5	Substance misuse education	1

		Health benefit
2.6	Information support to carers	2
2.7	Respite/day care	2
2.8	Detection/treatment of depression	2
2.9	Counselling	2
2.10	Supported housing	2

Cancers

3.1	Home-based palliative care	3
3.2	Specialist teams	3
3.3	Skin cancer prevention	1
3.4	Early recognition of skin cancer	2

Circulatory diseases

4.1	Cardiac rehabilitation	2
4.2	Stroke rehabilitation	2
4.3	Targeted stroke prevention	3

Mobility and the senses

5.1	Care attendants	0
5.2	Community orthopaedic clinics	1
5.3	Knee replacement	2
5.4	Community rehabilitation	1
5.5	Preadmission clinics	1
5.6	Equipment/aids	3
5.7	Mobile retinopathy screening	2

Infection and internal disease

6.1	Asthma education	2
6.2	Sex education	2
6.3	Community needle exchange	2
6.4	Parent/carer oral health	1
6.5	Targeted oral hygiene	1

Pregnancy and the newborn

7.1	New maternity care	0
7.2	Education/contraceptive clinics	3
7.3	Assisted conception	0
7.4	Folic acid	3
7.5	Paramedic obstetrics	1

		Health benefit
Other health programmes		
8.1	Waiting times/access	2
8.2	Child protection training	2
8.3	Child protection assessment	2
8.4	Smoking advice training	2
8.5	Dietetics training	1
8.6	Communication service	3
8.7	Domiciliary care	2

Appendix E Other benefits

Programme/option	Equity	Choice/ responsiveness	Personal responsibility	Access/ wait	Access/ local
Injury					
1.1 Mixed crew trials				✓	
1.2 Immediate care					
1.3 Community first aid			✓		
1.4 A & E	✓			✓	
1.5 Multiagency prevention	✓		✓		
1.6 Prevention information					
1.7 Safety aids	✓		✓		
1.8 Trauma centres				✓	
Mental health					
2.1 Community teams		✓			✓
2.2 LBHUs		✓			
2.3 Home/day detoxification			✓		
2.4 Brief interventions			✓		
2.5 Substance misuse education			✓		
2.6 Information and support to carers	✓	✓	✓		
2.7 Respite/day care		✓	✓		
2.8 Detection and treatment of depression					✓
2.9 Counselling		✓	✓		✓
2.10 Supported housing		✓	✓		
Continued					

Programme/option	Equity	Choice/ responsiveness	Personal responsibility	Access/ wait	Access/ local
Cancers					
3.1 Home-based palliative care		✓			✓
3.2 Specialist teams		✓			
3.3 Skin cancer prevention			✓		
3.4 Early recognition of skin cancer				✓	
Circulatory diseases					
4.1 Cardiac rehabilitation		✓			✓
4.2 Stroke rehabilitation		✓			✓
4.3 Targeted stroke prevention	✓		✓		
Mobility and the senses					
5.1 Care attendants		✓	✓		✓
5.2 Community orthopaedic clinics		✓			✓
5.3 Knee replacements				✓	
5.4 Community rehabilitation		✓			✓
5.5 Preadmission clinics					
5.6 Equipment/aids			✓		✓
5.7 Mobile retinopathy screening					✓
Infection and internal disease					
6.1 Asthma education			✓		
6.2 Sex education			✓		
6.3 Community needle exchange					
6.4 Parent/carer oral health	✓		✓		
6.5 Targeted oral hygiene	✓		✓		
Pregnancy and the newborn					
7.1 New maternity care		✓			✓
7.2 Education/ contraceptive clinics	✓		✓		
7.3 Assisted conception	✓	✓			
7.4 Folic acid			✓		
7.5 Paramedic obstetrics					✓

Continued

Programme/option	Equity	Choice/ responsiveness	Personal responsibility	Access/ wait	Access/ local
Other health programmes					
8.1 Waiting times/access				✓	
8.2 Child protection training					✓
8.3 Child protection assessment					✓
8.4 Smoking advice training			✓		
8.5 Dietetics training			✓		
8.6 Communication service	✓	✓	✓		
8.7 Domiciliary care		✓			✓

Appendix F Stakeholder consultation results

1 Ranking of injury options for change

Options	Total	General practice	Professional advice	Mean score CHC and local authorities	Hospital and community health services	Social Services	Councils of Community Service
Base	72	34	11	9	8	3	1
Trauma centres	2.5	2.6	2.4	2.6	2.4	1.3	3.0
Accident and emergency	2.0	1.8	1.9	2.8	2.3	1.7	3.0
Mixed crew trials	2.0	2.2	1.7	1.9	1.7	2.3	1.0
Community first aid training	1.9	1.9	1.7	2.1	2.3	1.3	2.0
Loan of sale of safety aids	1.7	1.5	1.7	1.3	2.0	2.0	2.0
Immediate care training; crash-call GPs	1.6	1.5	1.3	2.0	1.9	2.0	3.0
Multiagency accident prevention	1.5	1.4	1.5	1.4	1.4	1.7	2.0
Information for accident prevention	1.3	1.3	1.3	1.4	1.4	1.0	1.0

(Mean scores: high = 3, medium = 2, low = 1)

2 Ranking of mental health options for change

Options	Mean score						
	Total	General practice	Professional advice	CHC and local authorities	Hospital and community health services	Social Services	Councils of Community Service
Base	72	34	11	9	8	3	1
Increased respite and day care	2.5	2.3	2.6	2.8	2.7	2.3	1.0
Community mental health teams	2.4	2.4	2.5	2.4	2.1	2.7	3.0
Improved information and support for carers	2.3	2.3	2.0	2.6	2.1	2.3	3.0
Counselling in primary care	2.1	2.3	1.9	2.3	1.3	2.0	2.0
Substance misuse education	2.0	2.1	1.9	1.7	2.0	2.3	1.0
Home and day detoxification	1.9	2.0	1.7	1.6	2.3	2.7	2.0
Improved detection/ treatment of depression in primary care	1.9	1.6	2.3	2.3	2.1	2.3	2.0
Supported housing	1.8	1.8	1.7	1.6	1.9	2.3	2.0
Brief interventions	1.7	1.7	1.9	1.2	1.4	2.3	2.0
Locally based hospital units	1.7	1.5	1.7	1.7	2.0	2.0	1.0

3 Ranking of cancers options for change

Options		Mean score					
	Total	General practice	Professional advice	CHC and local authorities	Hospital and community health services	Social Services	Councils of Community Service
Base	72	34	11	9	8	3	1
Home-based palliative care	2.5	2.4	2.6	2.4	2.8	2.7	2.0
Concentration of treatment in specialist teams	2.4	2.3	2.4	3.0	2.8	2.0	3.0
Skin cancer prevention	1.8	1.6	1.8	1.8	1.6	2.0	1.0
Early recognition of skin lesions	1.8	1.5	2.1	1.9	2.0	2.7	1.0

4 Ranking of circulatory diseases options for change

Options		Mean score					
	Total	General practice	Professional advice	CHC and local authorities	Hospital and community health services	Social Services	Councils of Community Service
Base	72	34	11	9	8	3	1
Community stroke rehabilitation	2.5	2.4	2.3	2.4	3.0	2.3	3.0
Cardiac rehabilitation	2.1	2.2	2.0	2.8	1.9	1.7	3.0
Targeted stroke prevention	1.8	1.5	2.3	1.9	2.0	2.7	3.0

5 Ranking of mobility and the senses options for change

Options	Mean score						
	Total	General practice	Professional advice	CHC and local authorities	Hospital and community health services	Social Services	Councils of Community Service
Base	72	34	11	9	8	3	1
Community-based rehabilitation	2.3	2.0	2.2	2.8	2.6	2.7	3.0
Care attendants	2.1	2.4	1.8	2.4	1.8	1.3	1.0
Community-based orthopaedic clinics for older people	2.1	1.9	1.8	2.8	2.1	2.7	3.0
Increase knee replacements	2.1	2.0	1.7	2.6	2.4	1.3	3.0
Equipment/aids for disabled people	2.1	1.8	2.3	1.8	2.4	2.7	2.0
Preadmission clinics	1.9	1.9	1.6	2.3	2.1	1.3	2.0
Mobile retinopathy screening	1.7	1.8	1.5	1.4	1.9	1.3	2.0

6 Ranking of infection and internal disease options for change

Options		Mean score					
	Total	General practice	Professional advice	CHC and local authorities	Hospital and community health services	Social Services	Councils of Community Service
Base	72	34	11	9	8	3	1
Asthma patient education in primary care	2.2	1.9	2.5	2.7	2.1	2.3	3.0
Sex education in schools	1.9	2.1	2.0	1.1	1.8	2.0	1.0
Community-based needle exchange	1.8	1.6	2.0	1.4	2.0	1.7	2.0
Targeted oral hygiene education	1.8	1.7	1.7	2.0	1.9	1.7	3.0
Parent/carer education in oral health	1.6	1.6	1.6	1.4	2.0	1.3	2.0

7 Ranking of pregnancy and the newborn options for change

Options		Mean score					
	Total	General practice	Professional advice	CHC and local authorities	Hospital and community health services	Social Services	Councils of Community Service
Base	72	34	11	9	8	3	1
Unwanted teenage pregnancy: education/ counselling/ contraceptives	2.4	2.4	2.5	2.1	2.3	3.0	3.0
New models of maternity care	2.0	1.8	2.2	2.3	1.9	1.7	1.0
Preconceptual use of folic acid	1.9	1.9	2.1	2.1	2.0	1.7	1.0
Ambulance paramedic obstetric training	1.8	1.8	1.5	1.9	2.1	1.3	1.0
Assisted conception	1.5	1.7	1.2	1.0	1.3	1.7	1.0

8 Ranking of other options for change

Options	Total	General practice	Professional advice	CHC and local authorities	Hospital and community health services	Social Services	Councils of Community Service
				Mean score			
Base	72	34	11	9	8	3	1
Waiting times and access	2.6	2.8	2.0	2.8	2.5	2.3	3.0
Domiciliary care	2.0	2.0	2.0	1.7	2.0	1.7	2.0
Child protection: primary care training	1.9	1.8	1.8	2.3	2.0	2.7	1.0
Child protection: medical input to assessment	1.9	2.0	1.5	2.1	1.9	2.0	1.0
Communication service for ethnic minority patients	1.8	1.7	1.9	1.2	1.9	2.3	2.0
Smoking reduction: primary care training	1.7	1.8	1.7	1.4	1.5	2.0	1.0
Dietetics: training for primary care	1.5	1.5	1.5	1.6	1.6	1.3	2.0

9 Revised percentage for each programme area

(Participants were asked: 'What percentage share of the total expenditure by the health commission do you think should be allocated to each programme?')

Health programme				Mean (%)			
	Total	General practice	Professional advice	CHC and local authorities	Hospital and community health services	Social Services	Councils of Community Service
Base: All who disagree with current allocation	43	16	9	5	5	2	1
Injury	7.5	7.4	7.9	8.3	6.8	7.0	9.0
Mental health	16.5	17.5	17.4	13.8	15.8	17.5	17.0
Cancers	9.1	8.2	7.4	14.8	8.8	8.5	6.0
Circulatory diseases	12.3	11.9	12.4	11.3	14.0	13.0	11.0
Mobility and the senses	21.7	21.1	21.8	21.0	21.8	21.5	23.0
Infection and internal disease	26.6	27.1	27.3	24.3	27.0	26.5	30.0
Pregnancy and the newborn	6.4	6.9	6.0	6.8	6.0	6.0	4.0

10 Percentage of additional money would allocate to each programme area

(Participants were asked: 'If additional money becomes available, what proportion of it would you allocate to each programme?')

Health programme		Mean (%)					
	Total	General practice	Professional advice	CHC and local authorities	Hospital and community health services	Social Services	Councils of Community Service
Base	72	34	11	9	8	3	1
Injury	10.5	10.8	10.0	8.0	9.7	8.3	20.0
Mental health	18.3	18.9	18.9	9.8	20.1	18.3	15.0
Cancers	17.3	16.4	14.6	25.0	17.0	21.7	20.0
Circulatory diseases	16.9	15.9	15.7	16.7	20.9	21.7	20.0
Mobility and the senses	16.0	16.5	17.8	15.3	13.6	13.3	13.0
Infection and internal disease	13.7	14.5	15.3	16.7	7.0	10.0	11.0
Pregnancy and the newborn	9.6	9.6	9.5	8.5	12.7	8.3	1.0

Appendix G Expert panel: personal profiles

Professor Chris Ham

Chris Ham joined the Health Services Management Centre (HSMC), University of Birmingham, in 1992 and became Director in 1993. He has previously worked at the King's Fund College and King's Fund Institute and at the Universities of Bristol and Leeds. He has BA and MPhil degrees from the University of Kent and a PhD from the University of Bristol.

Chris has taken a special interest in health services since 1975, when he joined the staff of the Nuffield Centre for Health Services Studies at Leeds University. From Leeds Chris moved to the School for Advanced Urban Studies at Bristol University in 1977. He lectured there in health policy and management and published his second book, *Health Policy in Britain*, in 1982. This has since become a standard textbook on the NHS and is now in its third edition.

At Bristol, Chris developed his interest in working at the boundary between the academic community and the world of policy and practice. He also developed his research activities, publishing a fourth book, *Managing Health Services*, in 1986. This was based on research into the work of the Bath and Croydon Health Authorities and focused particularly on the role of health authority members in policy making.

Chris joined the King's Fund in 1986. At the Fund, he produced a number of briefing papers, research reports and articles on health policy issues. Chris specialized in work with chairmen and members of health authorities as well as developing a strong interest in the implementation of the NHS reforms and the development of the purchasing function. His sixth book, *The New NHS*, was published at this time.

Chris left the King's Fund in 1992 to take up a Chair in Health Policy and Management at the University of Birmingham. Within HSMC he leads a team of over 30 academic and support staff, concentrating on purchaser development, primary care development, board development and quality management.

Mr Frank Honigsbaum

Frank Honigsbaum is a senior research fellow at the Health Services Management Centre, University of Birmingham. He has written extensively on the history and operation of the NHS but is now concentrating on resource allocation as he sees the development of the purchasing function as the most difficult challenge facing the service. His recent publications include an exhaustive study of Oregon's controversial health rationing plan, an official study (with others) of the way six leading health authorities set priorities and (with others) a comparative view of the way five countries decide health care priorities.

Dr James Raftery

James Raftery worked with Wandsworth Health Authority from 1985 as in-house health economist. He was initially involved in option appraisal and capitation funding.

His focus shifted to purchasing in 1989. He became part of Wandsworth's strategic review team to 1993 and was involved in the development of price banding in contracts and in the application of health needs assessment. He continues as a part-time consultant to Wandsworth Health Authority.

James also worked part-time as economic adviser to the Department of Health on purchasing between 1990 and 1993. He was also an Honorary Senior Lecturer at St George's Hospital Medical School to 1993.

James is currently split between Wessex Institute of Public Health and the National Casemix Office. He is also an Honorary Senior Lecturer at the Department of Public Health Sciences, Southampton Medical School.

He has written various publications, most recently on the development of more sophisticated contracting and on capitation. He is the joint editor of the recent NHSME publication, a two-volume book, *Epidemiology Based Health Needs Assessment*, covering 20 diseases.

Professor Ray Robinson

Ray Robinson is Professor of Health Policy and Director of the Institute for Health Policy Studies at the University of Southampton. Before moving to Southampton in July 1993, he was Deputy Director of the King's Fund Institute. Earlier in his career he worked as an economist in HM Treasury and was a Reader in Economics at the University of Sussex. He has also held visiting posts at a number of universities in North America and Australia, has acted as a consultant to health authorities, government departments and international organizations, and has carried out assignments for management consultants in Britain and overseas. His work at Southampton is concerned with various aspects of health finance, economics and management and he has published widely in this field. He is the Vice Chair of East Sussex Health Authority.

Ms Jo Ash

Jo is Director of Southampton Council of Community Service, was previously Chief Officer at Eastleigh Council of Community Service and has over 15 years' voluntary sector experience including as a consultant working on women's health, disability advice and special needs housing issues. She has been a member of national association working groups on women's issues and voluntary sector funding. Her first degree is in Social Studies and more recently she completed an MA in State Policy and Social Change.

Dr Colin Godber

Dr Colin Godber has been a consultant in old age psychiatry in Southampton since 1973 and for several years doubled up as general manager. He has also acted as a consultant to WHO, the Institute of Health Services Management and the Centre for Mental Health Services Development. His choice of specialty reflects a long-standing interest in social factors in health and inequities in access and provision for such groups as the elderly and mentally ill. Practice in this field has required close partnership with primary care and social services and has provided much first-hand experience in the rationing and effective use of finite resources in the face of expanding need and demand. A major current concern is the risk to the equity of care for those with chronic illness and disability inherent in the otherwise desirable development of joint commissioning by health and social services departments.

Dr Lawrence Maule

Lawrence Maule has been a GP principal for six years, having completed his vocational training in Poole. He is one of six partners in a double-ended practice spanning the semirural coastal area between Lymington and Barton-on-Sea.

He is part of a close-knit primary health care team based at the Lymington end of the practice. He is also involved in a number of primary care-related areas:

• detoxification and rehabilitation of drug users

• clinical assistant for the maternity unit at Lymington

- endoscopist at the day case unit at Lymington.

He has recently become Medical Officer for a group of schools for children with special needs.

Dr Maule is particularly interested in promoting good communication and working relationships between professionals, patients and carers. He has been involved in a number of projects in this area, working in conjunction with the FHSA, social services and the Department of Geriatric Medicine, University of Southampton.

Mr Peter Lees

Peter Lees is Senior Lecturer in Neurosurgery and Honorary Consultant Neurosurgeon at Southampton University and Hospitals Trust. He has a particular interest in both operational and research in medical management; he is Clinical Director in Neurosciences at the Wessex Neurological Centre, and board member of the British Association of Medical Managers and specialty Working Group Leader for the Healthcare Resource Group Project in Neurosurgery.

Mr Len Doyal

Len Doyal is Reader in Medical Ethics at the London Hospital and St Bartholomew's Medical Colleges. This is the only senior appointment of its kind in medical education in the United Kingdom. He is a member of and formally advises the Research Ethics Committee for the local health authority, for which he also chairs a working party developing policies for equitable purchasing.

Before his present appointment, Mr Doyal was Principal Lecturer in Philosophy at Middlesex University, where he taught the philosophy of science and moral and political philosophy for over 20 years.

He has published extensively in all of these areas. His latest book (with Ian Gough), *A Theory of Human Need*, won The Gunner Myrdal Prize in 1992 and The Isaac Deutscher Memorial Prize in 1993. This book is widely cited in the literature on resource allocation within medicine.

Mr Doyal began teaching and writing about medical ethics in the early 1980s. Aside from resource allocation, his other interests concern problems about informed consent, selective non-treatment, impaired competence, confidentiality, reproductive ethics, non-compliance and procedural approaches to dealing with these and other issues of moral indeterminacy within clinical care. He is currently under contract to write *Clinical Ethics in Theory and Practice.*

Index